TOGETHER ON MISSION

Building Gospel-Centered Missional Communities

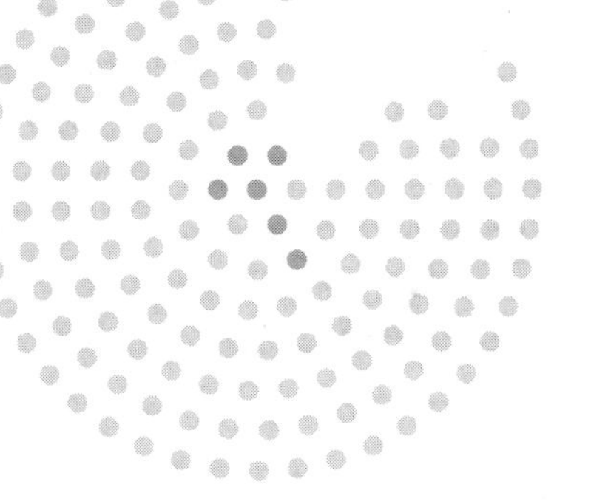

DANA **ALLIN** | DAVID **HANCOCK** | JIM **SINGLETON**

Published by Flourish (see *www.flourishmovement.org*).

We welcome your comments. Call us at 1-800-333-8300 or e-mail us at *editors@faithaliveresources.org.*

ISBN 978-1-59255-885-8

5 4 3 2 1

CONTENTS

Mission

Putting It All Together

INTRODUCTION

Why Another Missional Book?

Five hundred and eighty. That is the astonishing number of books Amazon.com lists with the word *missional* in the title, quickly confirming our belief that there really are a *lot* of books participating in the missional conversation. While we haven't quite read all of these missional books, we have read many of them, and we have been richly blessed by the way they have shaped our lives and ministry. The rich concept of a missional church is transforming churches throughout North America today.

Despite the number of books on the subject, some of you may not have heard the terms *missional* or *missional church*, so let's get up to speed on the subject. Every Christian knows that God has sent the church on a mission to bring the gospel of Jesus Christ. To accomplish that mission, the church may send out missionaries or evangelists to call people to faith in Christ. More recently, many churches have also sought to attract people to the church through its quality programs and relevant worship services. This is often called an "attractional" mission approach.

Over the past few decades, many church leaders have come to realize that the attractional model is inadequate by itself. God's mission isn't just about getting people into church; it's also about entering into the life of the world, like salt and light (Matt. 5:13-16). The church is itself a partner in God's mission to establish his kingdom on earth as it is in heaven. God's mission to reclaim the world in Christ is the very reason for the church's existence. Or, to put it as compactly as possible, the church doesn't just have a mission, it is mission. It is *missional.*

While many fine books have been written on this subject from an academic, inspirational, or theoretical perspective, what's missing is a brief, practical small group study that can move people into God's mission (particularly from a Reformed perspective).

So the three of us felt called to collaborate on a biblically and theologically grounded but very practical workbook that could offer a vision for a missional community. We wanted also to provide some reflection and useful exercises that can help people actually form missional communities.

What exactly is a missional community? There may be as many answers to that question as there are books through Amazon! For our purposes in this workbook we define *missional community* as "a group of people immersed in the gospel together on mission" (or "a group of Christians living out the gospel together in their community" or "a group of Christians engaged in God's mission together where they are").

Notice that there are three essential elements to this definition. First, a missional community must truly be a *community*. While there are individual aspects to our lives, we are not meant, as Christ followers, to live in isolation. We are stronger and more able to live out the good news of Jesus Christ when we are in community. Second, a missional community *lives out the gospel together*. That means more than just studying the Bible (though it certainly includes that). It means that the gospel saturates our life together so much that it shapes our total identity. The third aspect of the definition is that we are *on mission together*. In every aspect of life, a missional community seeks to partner with God's mission to bring about his kingdom on earth as it is in heaven.

Why Are Missional Communities So Important?

While *missional* could win the award for Christian buzzword of the decade, there are good reasons why understanding and applying this term are important. We have seen how missional communities have made a tremendous impact on the life of the church.

First, engaging people in missional communities is necessary in order to reach our world. While people will certainly still be reached through an attractional model of ministry, more and more people will not come in through the doors of your church even if it has the best programs and most meaningful worship in the world. So the church needs to go to them. Missional communities are the best way to reach individuals who would ordinarily never walk into a church building.

Second, engaging people in missional communities is one of the best ways to have Christians grow in their discipleship. The three of us have all had experiences with people who were faithful in worship and were involved in Sunday school, small groups, and other programs of the church—only to reach plateaus in their spiritual formation. But when they became involved in a missional community, they began to experience dramatic growth in their Christian maturity. God has formed us as communal beings, and when we become immersed in God's mission together, we will experience growth! Missional author Alan Hirsch asserts that when people begin to engage in missional ministry together, their latent missional DNA (mDNA), which is in us from conversion, is activated, and discipleship accelerates.

Finally, missional communities are one of the best ways to bring about revitalization in our churches. The transformation of existing churches is one of the most difficult challenges we face today. People have often approached the transformation of churches by changing logos, launching websites, adding contemporary worship services, and changing the church's vision and values statements. These are not bad practices, of course, but to really change an organization, the people in it must be changed. If even 5 to10 percent of an existing church can begin to live in dedicated missional communities, the whole congregation will begin to change. When new disciples share their stories within the church, it arouses the mDNA within others in a congregation. When individuals are changed, the culture of the church changes. And this creates the foundation and momentum for church transformation.

Forming a Missional Community

A missional community is different from a typical small group ministry in the church. Small groups are meant to build discipling relationships among Christians who study God's Word together, which is a fine goal. But by its very nature a small group will tend to value intimacy over drawing new people into its community. A missional community, on the other hand, forges authentic relationships as members immerse themselves in gospel-centered, outwardly directed mission together.

This workbook lays out an intentional process for the formation of missional communities. Moving in a missional direction requires important changes to our typical understanding of ministry. Each of the sessions in this book will introduce a new concept, beginning with a brief introduction and followed by an in-depth Bible study on that concept. Finally, a series of discussion questions will help the group discover practical ways to apply that biblical concept in the following week.

The book is divided into five sections. The first section provides an understanding of what it means to be missional and how missional communities should see themselves as micro-expressions of the whole church.

The next three sections explore the three elements of missional community in our definition "a group of people immersed in the gospel together on mission." The *Gospel* section focuses on what it means to be immersed in the gospel by exploring how our God-given identity can penetrate deep into our hearts and mold our identity, motivations, and actions. The *Community* section focuses on the dynamics of biblical community and how these might differ from the ways we may have experienced community in the past. The *Mission* section explores what it means to be truly on mission together by discovering how our community can be a conduit to facilitate the kingdom of God on earth. We will see how the mission of God encompasses both spiritual *and* physical renewal—in other words, focusing on both evangelism *and* justice.

The final section will help the community, individually and corporately, discover its own particular rhythms of communal and missional life. It will enable the group to discover to whom they are sent as ambassadors of Christ, and how they will disciple and nurture one another in faith.

Getting the Most Out of This Process

The process of forming missional communities is exciting! But there will be times when your group runs into challenges and either pushes back or slips into being a group that studies *about* missional community rather than forming themselves *into* a missional community. Three things can help solidify success in the formation of missional communities.

First, we encourage you to meet once a week while going through this material together. If you apply the principles presented in this study, it will begin to change the rhythms of your life. But if there is not consistency in your meetings, these new practices will not become ingrained.

Second, you may find that some lessons will require more than one meeting to complete. Build some flexibility into your schedule. We suggest that while there are 20 sessions, you may want to schedule 24 weeks to go through the process so that you can have some extra time here and there to allow God to shape you and your group as you engage with powerful and challenging ideas for change or transformation. You may also find that you need a week every so often to review and crystallize what you have learned. Follow the Spirit's leading in your group.

Third, the most effective way to use this material is to have a trained missional leader coach walk alongside the leader of the group. We in Flourish have a process in which missional community leaders come together for a one-day orientation and then receive monthly coaching during the formation of their community. This process can help leaders navigate through the challenges of forming a missional community and maximize the success of the group. A person could also simply engage the services of a coach while going through their own missional community formation. For a list of event and missional leader cohorts, see our website *www.flourishmovement.org*.

May God bless you as you go on this journey together.

—Dana Allin, David Hancock, Jim Singleton

THE CHURCH

Session 1

WHAT IS THE CHURCH?

BY DANA ALLIN

What is the church? It's interesting that our instinctive response to this question is to think of the place or the building in which the church meets. Or, if we're past that, we may still think first of what we do in corporate worship. After all, the Reformed confessions say that the marks of the true church are the true preaching of the Word and the right administration of the sacraments—which, of course, take place in public worship. Everything else in the church community seems to be of secondary importance to many congregations. For example, if someone asks, "How big is your church?" we are more likely to think of worship attendance than small group participation or the percentage of our people who are engaged in service ministries. We tend to talk about "going to church" rather than "being the church."

Even so, looking around the world, and increasingly in North America today, we actually see the church and the gospel of Jesus Christ growing through a multiplication of small communities. Sometimes these small communities do not even have what we would consider a public worship service! In his book *Forgotten Ways* missiologist Alan Hirsch illustrates this point with the rise of the church in China. Prior to the rule of Mao Tse Tung, the number of Christians in China was 2 million. Under Mao Tse Tung, church buildings were taken away and their leaders were killed, kicked out, or imprisoned. Christians could not meet together in groups of more than 15. But the number of believers after the rule of Mao Tse Tung was found to be 60 million—a *three thousand* percent increase in the number of Christians in China, despite the fact that this wasn't "church" the way we often think of it.

During my previous call as a pastor to Indian River Presbyterian Church, I spent some time preaching on what the church really is. God used our time studying his Word together to begin a new direction for our congregation. One of our active members, Mary, called to let me know she wasn't going to be at worship for the next three weeks. Her kids were working at a local coffee shop on Sunday mornings, and Mary and her husband, with their busy lives, wanted to spend as much time as possible with their kids before they left for college. We had a great talk, and I jokingly told her it was absolutely fine as long as she mailed in her offering!

Soon after we talked, Mary ran into someone she knew who was going through a difficult time. Her friend had some questions about Christianity and wondered if she and her husband could meet with Mary to discuss them. Mary, of course, said yes and let her friend know that she and her husband, Gary, would be at the coffee shop on Sunday morning. Mary indicated that their upcoming conversation alleviated her self-imposed guilt about not being at church!

The following Sunday, the four of them had a wonderful conversation. The couple asked if they could come next week and bring some friends along. The following week there were eight who gathered to talk together. On the third week there were twelve people, including Mary and Gary. They engaged in lively and deep discussions in that casual, nonthreatening setting. In that coffee shop, Mary and her friends struggled together to discover the meaning of the gospel and how to live it out in their everyday lives. This could not happen while sitting in a pew for a Sunday service.

After three weeks, Mary called me and said with a semi-apologetic tone, "I don't think I can come back to church right now. I feel that

God wants me to shepherd this group of new believers and seekers." As I gave her my blessing and promised I'd be praying for them, I had to ask myself if I truly believed what I had been preaching. Was this new group a church? Was this group a sufficient form of church in and of itself? I not only answered these questions in the affirmative, but I had to admit that this expression was probably a better form of church for these friends at this time in their development than on our Sunday morning gatherings. As a congregation, we publically celebrated what was going on with Mary, and it began to spark a passion. Some small pockets of people began exploring how to be more intentional about being the church in the environment where God had placed them, whether it was work, school, or even the gym. Though they were active in Sunday worship, some began to feel a nudge to move their small groups in a missional direction.

If we are going to understand the power and function of missional communities, we must shift our understanding that church primarily happens in a building for public worship. If a missional community functions correctly (see session 2), it truly can be an authentic expression of church in and of itself. In particular, as Jesus says, "Where two or three are gathered in my name, there am I among them" (Matt. 18:20). This isn't to minimize the role of public worship gatherings. If a church is planted by way of a missional community model, it ought to move toward developing public worship; there are a great number of advantages to being able to have public worship. However, we don't want to get into the mindset that we aren't church until we have public worship.

At Indian River Presbyterian Church we had an 8:00 a.m. service. It was the least attended service (especially on the Sundays after Christmas and Easter and when daylight savings time began each spring!). People always told me on those less-attended mornings, "Well, Pastor Dana, wherever two or three are gathered, Jesus shows up!" If that is what is really meant by this passage, then is it saying that God won't be with us unless there is at least one other person? Do we need to have a quorum of people to be present in order for Jesus to show up? Of course not! What Jesus is saying is that if two or three are gathered in his name, there is the body of Christ. There is the church!

After all, the church exists in many forms and sizes. For example, we know that the church is made up of all believers throughout the world. We celebrate this reality on worldwide communion Sunday. The church can also be a group of congregations that form a denomination or a network to help further their call to God's mission together. And of course the local congregation is the most familiar expression of the body of Christ. We often assume that the local congregation is the smallest unit of church. But as Jesus makes clear in Matthew 18, even when two or three are gathered in his name, there is an expression of the body of Christ. There is church.

If we begin to understand these smaller units of church as genuine expressions of the body of Christ, we will have the framework and capacity to unleash these groups to function in ways we haven't even imagined!

Study and Reflection

1. In what ways do individuals or congregations, explicitly or implicitly, indicate that church is what happens during a weekend service and that everything else is supplemental?

2. Read Matthew 18:15-20. How do verses 15-19 add to the evidence that in verse 20 Jesus is saying that even two or three people are an authentic expression of church?

3. What are the advantages of affirming smaller groups of people as authentically being church? How would your congregation look if smaller gatherings were commissioned as church?

4. What are the dangers of affirming smaller groups of people as authentically being church? What would need to be in place in order to avoid potential pitfalls?

5. What shifts would have to happen in your local congregation (with individuals and with the culture) to affirm micro-expressions of church?

6. How do you think the number of Christians in China grew during the rule of Mao Tse Tung from 2 million to 60 million when all of the known leaders were removed and large group worship was disallowed?

7. What are the ways in which smaller micro-expressions of church could reach people who wouldn't be reached through a church that attracted people only through programs?

Prayer

Share prayer requests with one another and commit to praying for three to five people whom you would like to see come to faith in Jesus.

Application

During the coming week, imagine you were not allowed to have church with weekend worship and programs. Imagine that your group doing this lesson would be your only expression of church and you wanted to reach 100 people for Christ in the next year. How would you go about it? How would you make sure the functions of church were happening within your community? Share your thoughts when you come back together next time.

Session 2

CORE PRACTICES

BY JIM SINGLETON

In Session 1 we wrestled with the important question *What is the church?* One thing we learned was that we all have a tendency to become enamored with the building where the church meets.

During a mission trip to India I once visited the Taj Mahal, the most breath-taking building I have ever seen. Shah Jehan built it as both a mausoleum and a monument to his beloved wife. There is a perplexing legend about this famous building. During the long process of building the Taj Mahal the emperor often visited the site. During his inspections he bumped into a dusty box that was constantly in his way. Finally one day he ordered, "Get rid of it!" At first the foreman protested, but the Shah insisted, so they threw it away. Only later did he discover that the box contained the body of the very woman the building was built to honor. The story may not be true, but it is certainly instructive. The building itself became so important that its real purpose became lost.

It's not that buildings are bad or wrong, and we can certainly appreciate the beauty and heritage of our places of worship. A church building houses a congregation, and it's the congregation that is the point of it all. Look at the first few chapters of Acts, that exciting story of the first days of the church, and you will realize that buildings are secondary. In Acts 2:42-47 we see a snapshot of a congregation that is contagiously filled with the Spirit. It has five characteristics, and not one of them requires a building.

(1) It Was a Learning Church

The passage begins with the phrase "they devoted themselves to the apostles' teaching." In his commentary on Acts, C. K. Barrett says that the word *devoted* means "persisting obstinately in something." For example, we may be devoted to our yards, to fishing, to the meticulous care of our bodies—and we will do whatever it takes to care about the object of our devotion.

These Christians were devoted "to the apostles' teaching." They had a real thirst for understanding their new and liberating faith in Jesus Christ. The first core practice of a church should be a hunger for God's Word. Sadly, studies show that most church members in America cannot name three of the ten commandments, and a majority of church members cannot name two of the four gospels. It is so interesting to realize that no one needed to force this devotion on the early church. No newsletter was required—they just wanted to know. Are we devoted to learning?

(2) It Was a Relational Church

The text goes on to say that the early Christians were devoted to "fellowship" and to "the breaking of bread." A few verses later we read that they broke bread "in their homes" and ate together "with glad and generous hearts." This seems to be a reference to both a common meal and to the Lord's Supper, which we know was first observed as part of a common meal. It clearly emphasizes the relational depth of the congregation at Jerusalem.

Growing up in the church, I thought that fellowship had to do with where two or three cookies were gathered together. But the word *fellowship* here means "living a common life together." To be truly relational involves a new level of hospitality and a deeper connection than we often experience. It also suggests significant involvement in small groups—in what could be called missional communities.

Years ago, I had a friend in grad school who was the pastor of a church of Pakistanis living in Kuwait. The church had no building and was not allowed to gather all together—no more than 50 in one place. Amazingly, the church had 10,000 members functioning entirely in small groups. Is your congregation a relational congregation?

(3) It Was a Worshiping Church

Notice that the early believers were devoted to prayer and awe-filled. Some of this took place at the temple, since, as Jews, they were in the habit of going to the temple at particular times for prayer. They were "filled with awe" (v. 43, NIV) as they worshiped—overcome by what God was doing among them. And they broke bread together, which, again, was a way of observing the Lord's Supper. All of this pictures a worshiping community of Word and sacrament whose focus was on praising God.

It's the God-focus that epitomizes worship. Sometimes after worship people will say, "I didn't get anything out of that." If worship is directed to God, then God is the only one who gets to say that. When God is the focus, our petty desires and selfish needs are swept away in devoted worship.

(4) It Was a Winsome Church

This early congregation attracted the favor or goodwill of the people. There is something truly winsome about being with a Spirit-filled Christian. This is one of the most remarkable features of this passage. Many people see Christians as only fussy and judgmental people. But here "the Lord added to their number day by day those who were being saved" (v. 47). Without forgetting that it was the Lord who added to their number, the passion and fellowship of this vibrant early Christian community must have been huge. Are people attracted to the Lord because of the vitality of your congregation?

(5) It Was a Generous Church

As a part of their newfound devotion to God and to one another, these early Christians began giving away what God had placed in their hands. The author notes, "They sold property and possessions to give to anyone who had need" (v. 45, NIV). The very practice of being in the presence of God naturally triggers the very generosity that exists in the person of God. A generosity of abundance flows from God, and that same abundance flowed through this early expression of the church. They even held things in common for the sake of helping those in need.

Devotion to God and each other makes for congregations that overflow with generosity. What would your church look like if it returned to these five essential characteristics of the church?

Study and Reflection

1. As you read Acts 2:42-47, what impressions jump off the page about how this congregation looked?

2. Look at a second snapshot that Luke gives us in Acts 4:32-35. What do these verses add to the picture of what can happen to a congregation?

3. What is the most memorable picture of a congregation or a group within a congregation that you have seen or known? What was the primary trigger for that expression?

4. What are the major issues or barriers that are keeping your congregation from becoming more like these snapshots of the early church?

5. How might you begin to see those barriers move and more of these expressions from Acts be established?

Prayer

Share prayer requests with your group and remember your commitment to pray for three to five people whom you would like to see come to faith in Jesus. Further, pray that this study group can begin to experience each of the five characteristics of the Acts 2 church.

Application

Focus on how each micro-expression of the church can move into these five aspects of being the church. Then imagine how even a handful of these missional communities might influence a larger part of the church to see what the church can become.

Session 3

"GOD'S MISSION HAS A CHURCH"

BY DANA ALLIN

Several years ago, I was a consultant with a church that was interested in assessing its overall health by using the Natural Church Development (NCD) evaluation tool. It became apparent that the most significant area of weakness for this particular congregation was an area that NCD classified as "need-oriented evangelism." This 200-member church was not training its people to share their faith, nor were they effectively meeting the needs of the community. As a result, new people were not coming to faith.

As we were discussing what this weakness meant for the congregation's health, one well-meaning elder spoke up and said, "But what if I don't want our church to become a thousand member church?" I certainly understood the man's concern but then asked him, "If God did desire for this congregation to grow to a thousand members, would you be willing to be on board if it meant 800 new people would come to know Jesus as Lord and Savior?" The man had no verbal response, but his body language clearly communicated that he didn't understand. Though we had worked together to recognize that numerical growth was not the main goal, healthy things (including churches) do grow! Judging by this elder's statement, the church was here for him and not for those who didn't yet know Christ.

Many of us can think of situations in which our local church wanted to maintain the status quo at the expense of mission. Sometimes there is a conscious push-back against a mission vision, but usually there is a subtler subversion of the mission. The mission of the local church will often sound good to people on paper, but complacency and fear often derail the pursuit of that vision.

I was once at a gathering of leaders where author Reggie McNeal was the keynote speaker. He used a phrase that has since forever changed my view of church. Reggie said, "Your church doesn't have a mission. God's mission has a church." He articulated this concept in several ways by explaining that the church isn't the end in and of itself. The church is the means to an end for God's purpose alone. He went on to say that the church is like an airport. An airport is necessary to get you where you want to go, but the goal isn't to go *to* the airport, the goal is to go *beyond* the airport to a conference, a vacation, or the home of someone you care about.

This simple statement about God's church on mission was a light bulb moment for me! My own congregation had just gone through an extensive time of determining our mission and vision. This exercise was useful, of course, but it now struck me as audacious to claim that *we* could develop a mission for the church. God already had a mission for our church, as he does with every church, and he has clearly laid out that mission in Scripture. While it was good for the church to articulate and own the mission, we now better understood that any vision is God's alone. And because it is God's mission, it is not optional—not even when it challenges the comfort of a congregation.

So what exactly is this mission of God in the world? And what does God's mission mean for our congregations, especially those that struggle with complacency? We can begin to discover God's mission by examining what humanity lost in the fall. Then, knowing that God, through his Son, Jesus Christ, and by the Holy Spirit, is working mightily to restore what was lost helps us begin to grasp how God is using our churches to further his kingdom in this world.

Three Elements of Wholeness

There are three elements of wholeness in our lives that have been distorted as a result of the fall.

Physical wholeness. God's original intention for his creation was that we were to live forever, have ample food, and be free of disease. The warning to Adam and Eve in the garden was that if they ate of the forbidden tree, they would die. While they did not die instantly, the process of bodily decay began to occur and the length of life became finite. We also learn from Genesis 3 that it would become harder to get food for sustenance. When we look around at our world, we can see many examples of the results of physical brokenness. People go hungry. We experience a myriad of diseases, from the common cold to cancer. We are plagued by horrific natural disasters.

Yet God is on mission in the world to restore physical wholeness to our world. We know he is working powerfully through the healing that Jesus brings and through those who answer the call to care for the sick, feed the hungry, and clothe the naked (see Matt. 25:31-46).

Wholeness with each other. God created us to be in relationship with each other. Yet immediately after Adam and Eve ate the fruit of the forbidden tree, there was discord between them—and a sign of more relational struggles to come. We see evidence of strife in the next generation when, out of jealousy, Cain kills Abel. The loss of relational wholeness persists, generation after generation.

Throughout the Bible we discover that God is continually at work to bring relational wholeness to individuals and groups of his people. For example, Scripture paints a picture of heaven in Revelation 5 in which people from every tribe, tongue, and nation are gathered together around the throne of the Lord. In Ephesians 2, Jesus is described as the one who has broken down the dividing walls between Jew and Gentile through his sacrifice on the cross. Paul also teaches in Galatians 3:28 that the oneness available in Christ overshadows the cultural differences that often divide.

Healing relationships are a priority for our Creator. As God's people, we are called to bring that same relational wholeness to the world. In many different ways, we are God's agents, both within the believing community and outside of it. We are called to racial reconciliation, to encourage marriages to thrive, to learn to forgive, to parent in love, and to stand up against oppression in our communities and throughout the world. We are called to love others because God first loved us.

Wholeness with God. When Adam and Eve ate of the tree of the knowledge of good and evil, they lost an intimate relationship with God. This broken relationship persists in our world today as people are alienated from God and rebel against his will. Our relationship with God as he originally intended it can be healed only through God's gift of Jesus Christ, who took on our brokenness and paid for our sin. Jesus has the power not only to remove sin but also to bring his righteousness into our lives.

The church is God's vehicle to restore wholeness between people and God. This happens through evangelism, as we share the good news of Jesus Christ with those who don't believe, and as we follow our call to strengthen believers in Christ by continuing to speak the gospel to those who already believe.

Missional Wholeness

The church, in all its expressions, must effectively engage in all three areas of God's mission toward wholeness. Sadly, the church has sometimes put physical and relational wholeness at odds against wholeness with God. Churches that are self-described as liberal or progressive have often placed high importance on meeting physical needs and joining the fight against oppression, yet have often perceived evangelism as narrow-minded and as imposing ideas on others. Conversely, churches that are self-described as evangelistic or conservative have been largely focused on spreading the good news while neglecting compassion and justice. Even worse, churches have minimized all three aspects of wholeness by being so wrapped up in their own entertainment and comfort that they give only lip service to the mission of God.

Missional wholeness calls for joining in God's passionate commitment to restore complete wholeness to the world. As we meet people's physical needs, we pray that someday they will follow Jesus. We pray that those who will accept Jesus as their Lord and Savior will discover a new passion for relational wholeness with others. We pray that as we join in the struggle against oppression and injustice, the world may see the gentle rule of God's kingdom.

Study and Reflection

1. In what ways have you seen churches allow a subculture of complacency to subvert their stated mission? What things can you do to ensure this doesn't happen with this missional community?

For questions 2-4, read Genesis 3:1-24 (the Fall) and Revelation 21:1-8, 22:1-5 (the Restoration).

2. How do you view the physical brokenness that results from the fall, and how do you see physical wholeness in the restoration? Think of ways in which God throughout Scripture brought physical wholeness to people. Where in Scripture do you see God calling his people to bring physical wholeness to the world?

3. How do you view the relational brokenness that results from the fall, and how do you see relational wholeness in the restoration? Think of ways in which God throughout Scripture brought relational wholeness to people and groups. Where in Scripture do you see God calling his people to bring relational wholeness to the world?

4. How do you view the broken relationship with God that results from the fall, and what is the picture of our relationship with God in the restoration? Think of ways in which God throughout Scripture brought wholeness between people and himself. Where in Scripture do you see God calling his people to help others have a restored relationship with God?

5. As you look at all three aspects of our mission (to bring physical wholeness, relational wholeness, and wholeness between people and God), where have you seen your church strong and weak? Where have you seen yourself strong and weak? What are the things that keep you or others from passionately pursuing all three areas of mission?

6. We pray in the Lord's Prayer, "Your kingdom come, your will be done, on earth as it is in heaven" (Matt. 6:10). We see a picture of heaven in Revelation 21 and 22. What would your world (community, city, neighborhood, business, schools, sports, civic organizations) look like if God's kingdom were manifest there as it is in heaven?

Prayer

Along with taking some time to share personal prayer requests, pray that God will open your eyes and heart to where his kingdom needs to be manifest on earth as it is in heaven. Pray for specific places and situations that God brings to your heart and mind.

Application

Set aside three days this week (they don't need to be consecutive). On the first day ask the Lord to show you how you can respond to a situation that needs physical wholeness—and then respond to that situation. On the second day ask the Lord to show you how you can respond to a situation that needs relational wholeness—and then respond to that situation. On the third day ask the Lord to show you how you can respond to a situation in which someone needs wholeness in their relationship with the Lord—and then respond to that situation.

Session 4

PRAYER MOTIVATED BY COMPASSION

BY JIM SINGLETON

When a congregation begins to focus on becoming a gospel-centered, missional community, a variety of changes become necessary. Change is never easy in congregations, and it happens only when a number of dynamics begin to occur—both human and divine. Matthew 9:35-38 highlights at least six important ideas to recognize when a congregation longs to change.

(1) The Eyes of Jesus

"When he saw the crowds, [Jesus] had compassion for them, because they were harassed and helpless, like sheep without a shepherd" (v. 36). Notice those first words—"When he saw the crowds." There are several words in the Greek language that describe seeing. This one conveys more than the basic physical function of the eyes; it refers to genuine noticing. Some of us see things but don't notice things. After my wife and I have visited someone's home, for example, she might ask me what I thought of the color of the draperies in a particular room. I will often ask, "Were there drapes in that room?" Is it possible that I could sit in a room looking right at draperies and not really see them?

Do we see people in the same way Jesus does? The first impact of this text calls for learning to see the people who are in front of us. Do we see neighbors, and children, and those who work around us? Becoming a missional church means we grow to see the world as Jesus sees it.

(2) How Jesus Saw Them

Jesus saw the crowd as "harassed and helpless, like sheep without a shepherd." Here two verbs describe what Jesus sees: people who are harassed and helpless. To be harassed means to be vexed, troubled, or annoyed. It is a word that suggests an anxious state of mind. To be helpless means to be hurled, thrown, cast down, scattered, and dispersed. These two words together present a picture that most people in that culture could see, if they were looking: sheep minus their shepherd. That would be like an office without management or like a classroom without a teacher.

How do you see those around you? Do you see the world around you as Jesus sees it? Do you see people vexed and scattered and struggling to find meaning in their lives? To have a passion for God's mission, we need to see people with the eyes of Jesus, in the way that Jesus sees them. Sometimes we are apt to think that non-believers are having the time of their lives. Yet if you look at the movies of this culture, listen to its music, and watch its television programs, you will soon recognize the troubled yearning, the abject brokenness of our society. Change begins to happen to us when we see people around us in the way Jesus saw them.

(3) The Compassion of Jesus

The third thing to notice in this passage is the compassion of Jesus. He hurt for the people he saw. Jesus was neither indifferent to their hurt nor approving of it. His whole ministry involved moving toward people with tremendous compassion. I believe that the greatest motivation for evangelism and mission is not guilt or compulsion or persuasive recruitment, but compassion. First, see the pressing need of the people around you. Then ask Jesus to awaken your compassion. When the compassion of Jesus grows greater in us than our fears of rejection, we will begin to change and become the congregation Jesus longs for us to be.

(4) The Plentiful Possibilities of Jesus

Beyond the pressing need of these lost sheep, Jesus also saw possibilities. Here the metaphor shifts from shepherding to farming: "The harvest is plentiful" (v. 37). Jesus saw people not only as harassed but also as ready to respond to the invitation to believe the gospel. Jesus saw not only the crying needs of those around him, but also how the kingdom of God would meet those needs.

In the late 18th century, both John Wesley and George Whitefield saw how changed social conditions of the Industrial Revolution had brought misery to many of the poor. Their Christlike compassion drew them to go where the people were—in the fields and industrial wastelands—rather than to wait for the people to show up at a dignified church. The movement that they helped to shape opened the eyes of the church at a time when it tended to focus on itself.

Do you see plentiful possibilities? There are so many unreached, dechurched, and underreached people around us. Jesus sees them as plentiful possibilities. Some people look at the culture and say, "Isn't it a shame." Others see possibilities. The harvest is plentiful.

(5) The Problem

"The harvest is plentiful, but the laborers are few" (v. 37). There are not enough people sharing the good news of Jesus with others. There are not enough congregations that have consciously entered into the dynamic joy of reaching lost people. In the United States, there are over 360,000 congregations, most of which are either stagnant or declining. Somehow, with plentiful possibilities all around us, most churches are not harvesting. The plain truth is that we don't have enough Christians who believe they are part of the harvesting. Almost every congregation I've ever visited has a mission statement that says their mission is to share the gospel with the lost, yet little evangelism with the lost is done.

This reality troubled the Danish church critic Søren Kierkegaard, who wrote a parable about it: A man was passing down the street when he noticed in the window of a shop a sign that read, "Pants Pressed Here." He paused and looked at his own pants, and they were quite wrinkled. He decided to stop at the shop and get his pants pressed. So he walked up to the counter and began taking off his pants. The clerk was quite shocked. He said, "What are you doing, sir?" The man said, "I want to have my pants pressed." The clerk replied, "Why would you ask for that?" The man replied, "Well, you are a business that presses pants, and I would like for you to press these pants." The clerk asked, "Why would you assume that we press pants?" The man said, "You have a sign in your window that says you press pants." "Oh," said the clerk, "you don't understand. We do not press pants here; we paint signs here—but we don't press pants."

This is a problem: we say we believe in evangelism—it is in most mission statements—but most churches are not really doing it.. The usual way people come to belief is when regular Christians are willing to share not only their story but also the story of what God has done for us in Jesus Christ. People take a long time to believe; often it is a slow process. The average time from hearing to belief is four years—through an average of five witnesses.

But Jesus says the major problem with the whole movement is not enough congregations focused on the harvest.

(6) The Plan of Jesus: Pray

Jesus' solution to this "labor problem" may surprise you. He does not write a book about it or even put his hearers on a guilt trip. He does not form a committee or practice high pressure recruiting. Jesus doesn't ask us to read a book or even be in this study group. Jesus asks us to pray that God, the "Lord of the harvest" will send more people and more congregations into the harvest field. You see, we are not in charge of the harvest; God is. The Lord of the harvest will do the recruiting through the power of the Holy Spirit. What we need to do is earnestly pray that God will move our hearts with the compassion of Jesus to enter into the harvest field.

Study and Reflection

1. What part of this passage is new to you?

2. As you ponder your own heart, how would you describe your compassion for those who are harassed and helpless? How might compassion grow in your heart?

3. Are there really "plentiful possibilities" for the gospel all around you, or is this world moving farther and farther away from Jesus?

4. How many great "harvesters" have you known? What gave them the freedom to join in the harvest?

5. How often have you heard congregations pray that they would be set free to enter the harvest? What ingredient might trigger your group to begin such a prayer even now?

Prayer

Share a range of prayer requests and then pray about the very idea of compassion for the lost.

Application

See if you can begin to notice people—at work, in your neighborhood, at school. Get to know them by name. Find out what you can about their lives. See what might awaken in your heart if you get to know them.

GOSPEL

Session 5

THE GOSPEL, BELIEF, AND THE HEART

BY DAVID HANCOCK

"If you confess with your mouth that Jesus is Lord and believe in your heart that God raised him from the dead, you will be saved" (Rom. 10:9, ESV). What does it mean to believe the gospel of Jesus Christ in and with your heart? When we think of our hearts, we typically think of our emotions. But when the Bible uses the word *heart*, it has a much deeper meaning. The heart, in the Bible, is considered the seat of our mind, will, and emotion. In other words, the heart is the center of our *knowing, applying,* and *experiencing*." I think true belief in the gospel in and with our hearts means that all of these areas are active as we go about our everyday living:

- *knowing* the gospel in our minds
- *applying* the gospel to our actions
- *experiencing* the gospel with our emotions

Consider what happens when one of these is missing:

- *Experiencing:* If we are only *knowing and applying* the gospel without *experiencing* the gospel, then we become what Jesus calls "whitewashed tombs" (Matt. 23:27). "Whitewashed tombs" are people who appear to have it all together on the outside but are dead on the inside, much like fruit that looks good on the outside but is rotten inside. If we never truly experience the gospel, we lack joy and perceive the Christian life as joyless duty. True belief produces joy.
- *Applying:* If we are only *knowing and experiencing* the gospel but not *applying* it, then we fail to obediently live the life to which God has called us. True belief produces obedience. When we aren't living obediently, it means that in that moment we don't believe it is worthwhile to trust Jesus as the Savior and authority over our lives. True belief changes the way we live.
- *Knowing:* If we are only *experiencing and applying* the gospel without *knowing* the gospel, then we fall into emotionalism and legalism. If we don't know the truth of the gospel, we become people who act and feel without the power of the gospel of Jesus Christ in our lives. In actuality, we are acting and feeling in response to a false gospel. True belief centers on the one and only true gospel of Jesus Christ.

True belief in the gospel involves actively bringing all three of these crucial aspects of belief together.

The Lord on the Throne of our Hearts

In the Bible, the heart is the *seat* of our knowing, applying, and experiencing the gospel. The word *seat* denotes a position of power and authority. So we can think of our heart as a throne or a control center. It is the place from which our thoughts, actions, and feelings originate. It is a place of authority and power. However, true authority and power come not from the throne itself but from the one who sits on the throne. So while the throne is the control center, whoever or whatever is the lord of the throne is the controller. The ways we think, act, and feel all depend on who commands our control center.

Our hearts are like empty thrones within us, searching for the one and only worthy King. When we say we believe the gospel, we are saying we trust Jesus to be the Lord of our hearts. What happens when Jesus sits down to rule our hearts? We become more like him as he begins to guide our thoughts, actions, and feelings.

Growth and the Lord of Our Hearts

There is a common misconception that we *become* Christians by believing the gospel but that we *grow* as Christians by trying harder. The reality is that one becomes a Christian *and* grows as a Christian through belief in the gospel. Belief in the gospel is central to our growth because belief in the person and work of Christ produces people who are becoming more like Christ. They trust Jesus as the Lord on their heart's throne. He is the One who has come to be with them, to teach them how to live, and to give them the power to live that way. As Tim Keller says, we never graduate from the gospel. It's not the ABC's but the A-Z's. It's not that there isn't effort on our part; there is! Our effort is in knowing, applying, and experiencing the truth of the gospel. We believe and we go to the good news of Jesus Christ so that the Holy Spirit might help us grow in our belief.

In Mark 9:24 a man says to Jesus, "I believe; help my unbelief." We are all growing in our belief, and the more we believe, the more like Christ we become. This also means that every time we sin there is a belief problem in our hearts: we are trusting in some other lord to rule over our hearts. When sin beckons, we need to recall the life-changing truth of the gospel and trust in Jesus as the Lord of our hearts. We have to understand that belief in the gospel is the only power that will really change us so that we become more like Christ. (*Warning:* We must be careful not to see the gospel as a tool. The good news of Jesus changes the way we think, act, and feel. But if we make the gospel a tool, then we make growth and salvation more important than our Savior.)

Let's look at some examples of how belief in our hearts changes us. Each of these is an example of knowing, applying, and experiencing the gospel.

- *Loving:* If we are having problems loving someone who is hard to love, we need to remember that we were unlovable before Jesus came in to change our own hearts and lives. Christ makes us lovable through his finished work on the cross, making the love of God real for us. When we grow to know God's love, then we too become able to love those who are unlovable.
- *Prayer:* If we are having problems spending time with God in prayer, then we may be struggling to believe that Christ came from the Father so that we can have an intimate and real relationship with the Father. We need to remember and believe that Jesus came to our sinful, broken world to suffer and die so that we can have a relationship with the Father. We may now call God our "*Abba,* Father" through the One who cried out, "My God, my God, why have you forsaken me?" (see Mark 14:36; 15:34; Rom. 8:15).
- *Giving:* If we know that we should give but are having a problem giving, then we may be struggling to believe that Christ gave up everything for us (Phil. 2:1-8). We need to believe in our hearts that Christ has given his life for our sake; we need to experience the forgiveness and the new, self-giving life he has made possible for us with God. Then we will have the power to give.
- *Sacrifice:* If we are at times having problems sacrificing, then in those moments we have lost sight of the fact that Christ sacrificed himself for us. When we, in faith, remember how Jesus has sacrificed for us, then we will have the power through Christ to make sacrifices for others.

Christian growth is not primarily about trying harder. It's about believing more. See Jesus as the Lord of your heart and make way for him to have authority over your life. Rely on him for the power to live the way he is calling you to live.

Conclusion

The purpose of this session is to teach us that believing the gospel in our hearts means that we know the gospel in our minds, we apply the gospel to the way we live, and we experience the gospel with our emotions. When we believe the gospel, we begin to trust Jesus as the Lord of our hearts who controls our thinking, doing, and feeling. He is our Savior, the One who also helps us grow more and more into the people God created us to be.

In the next three sessions, we will look at each aspect of belief (knowing, applying, and experiencing) in more detail. You may want to revisit this session material as we build on the image of Jesus ruling on the throne of our hearts.

Summary of Believing the Gospel

Knowing the Gospel

The word *gospel* means "good news." The gospel is not *advice* about what we should *do* but *news* about what has been *done* for us. The headlines read, "God has come into the world to save sinners." The subtitle reads, "Believe! The King is here, and he has brought his kingdom! Turn to him!" It's the greatest news the world could ever hear. How does God save sinners? Jesus, the Son of God, comes into the world to stand in our place so that we can stand with him in his place (Heb. 2:13-18; 4:14-5:10). He both lives for us and dies for us. He comes to make a two-part exchange of records with us. In the first part Jesus *takes* our record of sin, which results in his death on the cross, where he is crushed under the weight of the Father's wrath against our sin (1 John 4:10). In the second part of the exchange we are *given* the gift of Jesus' perfect sinless record (Rom. 3:21-22; 4:22-25; 2 Cor. 5:21), which results in being loved by the Father as much as he loves Jesus (John 17:23)!

Applying the Gospel

The good news is that the power of God's kingdom has come not only to save us but also to transform us, our church, our city, and the world through the person and work of Jesus Christ. We ought to be consistently reorienting our lives around the promises and implications of the gospel. The gospel is not only the power of God for our salvation, but it is also, through the work of God's Spirit in us, our only true source of growth and transformation. This means we never move beyond the gospel but rely daily on its transforming power, in step with the Spirit (2 Cor. 3:18; Gal. 5:25).

Experiencing the Gospel

We experience the gospel when our knowledge of the gospel overflows into our entire being. Jonathan Edwards said, "There is a difference between having an opinion that God is holy and gracious, and having a sense of the loveliness and beauty of that holiness and grace. There is a difference between having a rational judgment that honey is sweet, and having a sense of its sweetness" (Harold P. Simonson, *Selected Writings of Jonathan Edwards,* 2nd ed., p. 55). The same is true with the gospel; until we experience its beauty, we will never understand it. In order to experience the gospel, two things must happen. We must (1) be convicted of our sin and (2) discover and rediscover the depth of God's grace. Along with that we must have daily and weekly rhythms or disciplines that help us in being convicted of our sin and rediscovering God's grace.

Study and Reflection

1. What does it mean to believe in and with your heart?

2. Churches often stress one of these three areas of belief: knowing, applying, and experiencing. What would you say your church stresses? What do you typically focus on in your life? Has that particular emphasis caused problems for you—and if so, what are they? (For example, if you are lacking in knowledge, you may need to spend more time reading and studying the Bible.)

3. Can you identify some phony lords that have been controlling you and sitting on the throne of your heart? How have they been influencing your thoughts, actions, and emotions?

4. Do you see Jesus as the authority of your life? Where in your life do you need to listen to him?

5. Do you see Jesus as the power in your life? Where in your life do you need to rely on him?

6. Do you believe that Jesus is with you? If not, what is influencing you to keep him out of your life?

7. In the past, how have you understood spiritual growth? In what ways has this lesson helped you better understand growth?

Prayer and Application

Look for areas in your heart where you are struggling to believe. Share those with people and ask them to pray for you. Ask them to speak the gospel to you so that you may believe more and trust more in Christ.

Session 6

KNOWING THE GOSPEL

BY DAVID HANCOCK

What Is the Gospel?

The word *gospel* means "good news." The gospel is not *advice* about what we should *do* but *news* about what has been *done* for us. The headlines read, "God has come into the world to save sinners." The subtitle reads, "Believe! The King is here, and he has brought his kingdom! Turn to him!" It's the greatest news the world could ever hear. How does God save sinners? Jesus, the Son of God, comes into the world to stand in our place so that we can stand with him in his place (Heb. 2:13-18; 4:14-5:10). He both lives for us and dies for us. He comes to make a two-part exchange of records with us. In the first part Jesus *takes* our record of sin, which results in his death on the cross, where he is crushed under the weight of the Father's wrath against our sin (1 John 4:10). In the second part of the exchange, we are *given* the gift of Jesus' perfect sinless record (Rom. 3:21-22; 4:22-25; 2 Cor. 5:21), which results in being loved by the Father as much as he loves Jesus (John 17:23)!

This exchange is both a substitution and a sacrifice. *The perfect God stands in the place of the guilty rebel.* God the Son is *condemned* so that we can be *accepted.* God the Son *suffers* so that we can have *joy.* God the Son becomes an *orphan* so that we can become *sons and daughters* of God. God the Son becomes *sin* so that the Father can see us as *sinless.* He is *cast out* of the presence of the Father so that we can *come into God's presence.* He becomes a *slave* so that we can be *free.* He dies and rises to new life so that we can have new, *eternal life* in him (John 5:24; Rom. 6:4-11).

This exchange is a gift of love that is absolutely free and cannot be earned. However, as Timothy Keller points out in *The Prodigal God,* the default mode of the human heart is to function as every other religion suggests and try to earn a right standing with God. Our default is to rely on rules and strategies to show God that we are worthy of being loved and accepted. We see that God is up in heaven, so we try to climb up to him by living the way we think we should be living. But Christianity tells us that we can never climb up to God. Our good is never good enough. The good news is that God becomes human, comes down to us in Jesus Christ, and dies in our place, paying the price for our sin. And when we put our faith and trust in him rather than in ourselves, he makes us alive and lifts us up to the Father in heaven so that we might enjoy him and be in relationship with him. While the gift is free for us, the cost for God was high: the life of God's only Son.

What we have to understand is that we either approach God with our record or with Christ's record. We have to pick one. If we pick our record, we are *guilty and condemned.* If we pick Christ's record, we are *loved and accepted.* Even after we become Christians, we still fall into this faulty way of thinking and living, which can drain us of the joy we have in Christ. Even though we are Christians, we can begin to function as if we aren't. If I ask, "What does God think of you right now?" people will typically think first about their own record. But for someone who truly understands what Jesus has done for them, this question will bring a smile to their face. Why? Because they know God loves them as he loves his one and only Son, and that truth has become very real to them. Do you understand the magnitude and beauty of the perfect record you are given in Christ? It is essential that we reorient ourselves with the gospel every day. The good news is that we are not only saved but also being transformed to live new lives now. The gospel gives us joy instead of guilt, and freedom instead of slavery. Let's expand on this good news by answering some questions about God, sin, Jesus, and faith.

Who Is God?

The Bible teaches that there is one God and there is nothing else like him. He is ultimate. He is radically different because he is the creator while everything else is his creation. However, God created human beings different from the rest of creation. God created us in his image (Gen. 1:26-27), and he did this in a very personal and intimate way by breathing life into the first man (Gen. 2:7). The God of all creation has designed us to know him in a very personal way. Not only are you God's, but he is yours (Jer. 30:22). He is our God who is both cosmically glorious and yet wonderfully intimate with us. He is of heaven, and yet he is our Father. He is holy and yet also loving. He is powerful and yet gentle, merciful and yet just, beyond our knowing and yet making himself known. His beauty exceeds our imagination, and yet he puts his beauty on display. He is infinite, and yet he shows himself in time. He is dependent on no one, and yet he is dependable. He is perfect and yet gracious, wrathful and yet good. He is all knowing, wise, and trustworthy. He speaks, and the cosmos listens—from the tiniest of cells to the largest of solar systems—and there is no place in the universe you can go that he hasn't created and where he isn't present. You will never meet anyone more loving and more terrifying, more tender and more to be feared. And he is right in being all of these. He is perfectly all of these.

Our God is one God in three persons: Father, Son, and Spirit. We tend to think that God created us and the world because he was lonely and wanted someone to love, but that is not the case. God is love and has always experienced perfect love and community within the Trinity. Creation is really an overflow of God's perfect beauty, love, and community within the Trinity. Creation is also an overflow of God's perfect power, authority, and control.

We were created by God in his image to be in relationship with our perfect God, to be in his perfect presence, and to see him as ultimate in our lives. We are meant to love God, enjoy him, glorify him, worship him, and obey him. If this sounds weird to you or gives you an uneasy feeling, there is a simple explanation for why you feel that way: sin and the fall. I realize that this is potentially offensive, but deep down I think we know it is true. We realize that things are not the way they are supposed to be. The Bible is very realistic about that, and it has an answer. Sin has caused us and the world to fall away from God.

What Is Sin?

The Bible tells us that everyone has sinned (Rom. 3:23)—absolutely everyone. Some of our sins we are aware of, and some of our sins we are oblivious of. Sin involves living in a way that is not in line with the way we were created to live. When we sin, we turn away from doing the things God has created us to do, and we live in ways that oppose the way God created us to live. We were created to see him as our Father, Creator, and King. Our sin is a rejection of God's Fatherly love, a denial of him as our powerful Creator, and a rebellion against him as our King who has control and authority over us. *In our sin we live as if we don't have a Creator. We try to find our ultimate joy in anything other than God. Sin gives us excessive desire for anything other than God. Sin is even lawlessness (2 Cor. 6:14), adultery against God (Jer. 3:6-8), cosmic treason toward God (as R. C. Sproul puts it in* The Holiness of God*; Gen. 3:5), and hatred of God (Rom. 8:7).* Does that sound harsh? That is what the Bible tells us. The Bible calls all of us enemies of God outside of Christ (Rom. 5:10).

Every time we sin we are tempted with the notion from Satan that says, "You can be like God" (Gen. 3:5). In other words, we are tempted to believe that we deserve the worship and glory God receives, that we deserve to be the ruler of our lives, and that we can find our desires, satisfaction, and identity fulfilled in something other than God. When we sin, we believe those words to be true. They allure us; they make us desire to remove God from his throne so that we can sit there ourselves. We want our own thrones, so we rebel against him as King. We don't want to depend on God but to be autonomous, so we reject him as

Father. We want to be in control, but God says, "No, I'm in control," and we hate him for it (Rom 8:7). Not only have we failed to love God and others; we have hated them. While our sins may seem small to us, in the eyes of God they are heinous. And when we understand what sin is, it will cause us to tremble in the presence of a perfectly holy God.

The Bible tells of a vision in which Isaiah comes into the presence of our holy God. He responds with these words: "Woe is me! For I am lost; for I am a man of unclean lips, and I dwell in the midst of a people of unclean lips; for my eyes have seen the King, the Lord of hosts!" (Isa. 6:5). What is going on here? Isaiah is so aware of his sin because he is in the presence of God. He is feeling the weight of his sin because God's anger toward his sin is pressing in all around him. In the presence of other sinners we don't seem so bad, but in the presence of the perfectly holy God we become very aware of our sin, and then we understand more of what it means to fear God.

What Are the Results of Our Sin?

Our sin results in our *condemnation* and *death*. First of all, we are *condemned* (Rom. 5:16, 18; 8:1). We are declared guilty. Second, our sentence is *death* (Rom. 6:23)—spiritual, emotional, social, and eventually physical and eternal death. All around us we can see the results of our own sin and of the sin we inherited from Adam (Rom. 5:12, 16). Look around. The world is in decay. There is suffering, loneliness, emptiness, shame, brokenness, and meaninglessness. In God's perfect presence these problems don't exist, but our sin has brought about a separation between us and God (Isa. 59:2). We see physical death all around us. And ultimately our sin results in eternal death. The Bible calls this hell. The fall of mankind into sin has caused us and the world to groan for something better, to groan for creation to be restored (Rom. 8:19-22). The world knows something isn't right. The Bible tells us we have been removed from Eden (the perfect presence of God), and creation longs to be restored. We know things are not the way they are supposed to be because we somehow and in some way remember Eden. We long to be home with God, where all things are right. We are in bondage to this corrupt world, and we are groaning for freedom.

How Do We Deal with the Problem of Sin?

There are three ways we try to deal with our problem of sin and the fall. We either (1) try to fix the problem through moral effort, (2) try to find things of this world to satisfy our longing, or (3) try to escape. Through moral effort we desperately try to justify ourselves. We try to be as good as we can so that God will love and accept us (Rom. 10:3). But the Bible tells us we can't do anything good outside of Christ (John 15:5). D. A. Carson in his book *For the Love of God* says, "Religious cant often hides not only ungodly behavior, but a secret lust to do evil." In other words, we might follow all the rules and look good on the outside, but our motives on the inside are always wrong if we do not remain in tune with Christ. This is our failed attempt at self-justification.

Second, we try to satisfy our longing for God with other things such as money, power, sex, fame, comfort, control, careers, approval from others, hobbies, love, and more. The Bible calls this idolatry. We take good things in God's creation and make them ultimate by trying to find our identity in them, but they never seem to deliver. In fact, our hearts are crushed, abused, and ultimately taken over by these tyrannical idols. The problem with idolatry is that what we idolize is never the real thing. They are good things that were never meant to be ultimate. Only the real thing can deliver. Any attempt to find satisfaction, fulfillment, and meaning outside of Christ will fail.

Third, we might try to escape or stuff down our lack of contentment by indulging in desires, distractions, and giving undeserved glory to ourselves and/or the things of this world.

The really bad news for us is that there is nothing at all we can do about our sin and its results. We are helpless on our own. We can't be good enough, search far enough, or escape deep enough. Eventually our sin will catch up with us. St. Augustine explained that actually, outside of Christ, we can do nothing but sin. We are in desperate need of help. We need a deliverer.

Who Is Jesus, and What Did He Do?

(How does God deal with the problem of sin and death?)

What we have to understand is that because God is perfectly just, he can't simply forget our sin; he has to deal with it. So how does God deal with our sin? In eternal love, before the foundation of the world, the triune God had a plan to save humanity. The Bible is the story of that plan. In the Bible we see that the Father ordains the plan of salvation, the Holy Spirit makes the plan known to us through Scripture, and Jesus is the one who accomplishes the plan. That is why all of Scripture points us to Jesus. He is the plan of deliverance. The Bible is the story about Jesus and how he saves his people. Let's look at how God accomplishes this plan through who Jesus is and what he did.

The Incarnation

In the incarnation God enters into his own creation. In the incarnation we see God come to do three things: (1) to be with us, (2) to live for us, and (3) to die for us. In God's coming to be with us we see that "the Word became flesh" (John 1:14). Jesus is "God with us" (Matt. 1:23). He came, bringing his kingdom, to tell us who he is and what he came to do. He came to teach us about the Father, about the Spirit, about himself, and about his kingdom. Second, Jesus came to live the life we should have lived (Gal. 2:20). In order for the exchange to work, Jesus had to hand over a perfect record to us. What is interesting is that while Adam was pursued by Satan to be tempted, Jesus went out to be tempted by Satan and to remain obedient to God on our behalf (Matt. 4:1). Jesus was tempted in every single way but remained sinless so that he could claim victory for us (Heb. 4:15). Through faith we are given his record and are joined to his victory. Jesus did not come to prove himself strong and Satan weak, but to seal our victory over sin. For us, Jesus lived the life we should have lived; therefore, we share in his victory in the same way we have shared in Adam's defeat. Third, Jesus came as a human being to die our death and deliver us from the evil we have become a part of (John 3:16-21). Jesus came as both God and man so that he might taste death in his humanity and overcome death as God. He submitted to dying by becoming human; yet he overcame death in his divinity.

The Cross

Just before Jesus embraced the cross, he was deep in prayer with his Father. He prayed that God would let this cup pass from him; yet he also submitted to drinking the cup (Luke 22:41-44). Here we see a picture of both his humanity and his divinity. In his divinity he is obedient. In his humanity we see him so worked up that he is sweating blood, a phenomenon that actually can happen if someone is under enough stress. The question before us is, What was Jesus so stressed about? Was it the physical suffering he was about to endure? Was it the emotional suffering? No, it was the spiritual suffering. The cup represents God's wrath for the sin of mankind. On the cross Jesus drinks the cup of God's wrath so that we don't have to. Scripture tells us that Jesus actually becomes sin on the cross (2 Cor. 5:21), and as he becomes sin he is crushed by the wrath of his own Father. He swallows the judgment that was meant for you and me. This was the only way our redemption could be bought. And Jesus bought it for you. He had you in mind when he purchased redemption (1 Cor. 6:20). The kingdom of God has come through the King's suffering.

At the cross we see the climax of the gospel story: the Son of God is crucified and cursed so that mankind can live and be blessed. The world is turned upside down and pulled inside out—so much so that the curtain of the temple is torn in two (Matt. 27:51). The curtain of the temple was the way into God's presence (Heb. 9). It symbolized the way back to Eden. And when the curtain was torn in two, that meant sinners now have access to the throne of God and can walk in through faith. When Jesus cries out the words "It is finished" (John 19:30), redemption is accomplished. We are given the gift of his record, and he takes from us our record.

When Jesus says on the cross, "Father, forgive them, for they know not what they do" (Luke 23:34), he is saying, in effect, "Father let me pay their debt in order to buy their forgiveness. Punish me, God—not them." Do you see what happened here? *We* crucified Christ. What we meant for evil in crucifying Christ, God meant for our good (Acts 2:22-36). On the cross God's infinite love and holiness collided. Through the cross God displayed his perfect love and justice. And when God's perfect love and holiness collided on the cross, the kingdom of God was opened to us. The tension of coming into the presence of God was removed, and now we can stand before the holy God guiltless, carrying the record of our Savior.

The Resurrection

Three days after Jesus breathed his last breath on the cross, he conquered sin and death by breathing again. In the resurrection Jesus claimed both his divinity and our eternal life. The resurrection is good news because through it Jesus laid sin and death in the grave. Christ has risen, and our union with him means that the same is true for us. Through faith we are united to him and made into a new creation that is fully alive. Though we were dead, now we are made alive (Rom. 6:5-11; Eph. 2:4-10). The resurrection means that eternal life begins now. Death has been undone, and eternal life starts now!

The Ascension

Where is Jesus now? Jesus is at the right hand of the Father ruling and reigning as King. He testifies on our behalf that we are his and he is ours (Rom. 8:34). This tells me that when I stand before the Father and meet God face to face, Jesus will turn to the Father and say, "He is mine and I am his; I lived the life that this man owed you, and I died the death that this man deserved. I took the record of this man and gave him my record." And the Father will look at me and say, "You are my beloved son, with whom I am well pleased." For each one of us who believes in Christ as Savior, these words ring true.

The Return

Jesus promises that one day he will return in all his glory to make all things right and new (Rev. 21:1-5). When Jesus first entered into creation, he came as the servant King to die for our sins, but one day he will come as our exalted King in all his unveiled glory. When he comes, heaven and earth will be made new and perfect, and the kingdom of God will be fully here. God will wipe away every tear from our eyes and all the sorrow in our hearts. There will no longer be mourning, death, or pain. Scripture tells us that the affliction we feel in this life is actually preparing us for the eternal glory in which we will one day live when Christ returns. We grow in faith and hope by looking not to what is seen, because that will one day fade away, but to what is unseen, because that is what awaits us in eternity (2 Cor. 4:17-18).

How Should We Respond to the Gospel?

Scripture calls us to put our faith fully in Christ. When we have faith in Christ, it means that when we stand face to face before the Father, we offer up not *our record* but *Christ's record*. We turn to Christ as our Savior and place our trust fully in him, not in ourselves. And as we fix our eyes on our Savior, in whom we trust, he gives us a desire to turn away from sin because we are being drawn toward the saving love of Christ in the forgiveness of our sins and the gift of a new record. This is what the Bible calls repentance.

Repentance isn't just a one-time thing but something we do daily. And as we daily fix our eyes on Christ, the Holy Spirit gives us the desire to turn away from our sin. Satan has lured us away from God, and Jesus comes so that we might fix our eyes back on him and turn away from our sin. He offers us a grace that is absolutely irresistible, and it is through this grace that we are drawn away from our sin and to our Rock and Redeemer. This means we go "all in" with Christ every day. It means that every day we are reorienting our lives to trust more in Christ.

It's not that we won't sin again when we come to Christ. We will struggle with sin till we die. When we first put our trust in Christ, we are saved from sin's dominance but not its influence, as John Owen puts it. We are saved for all of eternity, but sin still influences us in this life. But when we turn and trust in Christ daily, he is saving us each day from sin's influence more and more. By faith Jesus is delivering us daily from the evil one who is luring us and influencing us to live a life of fear, shame, doubt, and hopelessness. When we daily turn to Christ, we are rescued more and more from sin's influence, and we learn to live more and more the way our Savior is teaching us to live.

What Are the Promises We Receive Through Belief in the Gospel?

Through the person and work of Christ all the promises of the Bible to God's people come true (2 Cor. 1:20). These promises are given by the Father and made known to us by the Holy Spirit. What are these promises?

Well, we are promised that the power of God's kingdom has come to save and transform our individual hearts and lives and our world through the person and work of Jesus Christ. The kingdom is here now but is not yet fully revealed. We are promised a new life in Christ in which we are given a new heart to trust, love, and follow Christ (1 Pet. 1:3). We are now co-heirs with Christ (meaning all that is his is ours) through our union with him (Rom. 8:17). In this union we are blessed with every single spiritual blessing (Eph. 1:3). We are sinners who are given the gift of Christ's perfect record (Rom. 5:1). We are adopted sons and daughters (Eph. 1:5) who are loved by the Father as much as he loves the Son (John 17:23). This means there is nothing we can do or not do that will cause God to love us more or less. We are promised that we will become more and more like Christ each day (2 Cor. 3:18; 1 Thess. 5:23-24). In other words, you will become more and more like the person God has called you to become in eternity. We are also promised that one day, when Christ returns, he will bring his kingdom fully. Then we will see Christ just as he is, and then we will become like him (1 John 3:2). When that happens, we will no longer be able to sin but will reflect him and his glory perfectly. We are also promised that one day we will dwell with God perfectly (Rev. 21:3). We are promised a room in our Father's house that is prepared for us by Christ (John 14:2). There will be a new heaven and new earth (Rev. 21:1), where we will live fully as God's people and experience him fully as our God. All things will be made right, death will be no more, and we will experience the perfect joy that is found only in God (Rev. 21:4).

Study and Reflection

1. Have you truly put your faith in the good news of Jesus Christ? If not, what is holding you back? If you are ready, ask those in your group to help you in putting your faith and trust in Christ.

2. How has this session helped you grow in your faith and/or better understand your faith?

3. What part of the gospel do you better understand?

4. What part of the gospel do you find difficult or hard to understand?

5. When you forget the love and acceptance you have in Christ, what are some of the things you do to try and earn God's love and acceptance?

6. How do your church, family, and friends measure God's love and acceptance of them? What can you do to help them better understand the gospel?

Prayer and Application

Pray that God will help you see the beautiful gift you have been given in Christ and live each day enjoying the love and acceptance you have received from Christ.

Session 7

APPLYING THE GOSPEL

BY DANA ALLIN

Adoption in Christ is a very powerful biblical concept for me. I am not only adopted as a child of God but was also adopted by my parents. My birth mother and father were both 17 years old and lived in a small community in Iowa. When my birth mother became pregnant, she was sent to live with her aunt and uncle in Santa Barbara, California. The nurse at her obstetrician's office lived next door to my adoptive parents, and she knew they wanted to adopt a child. The nurse connected them with my birth mother, and she decided that they should be the ones to adopt me. My adoption was always presented very positively in that I had two families who loved me. I have never met my birth parents, but I have a letter from my birth mother telling how she loved me enough to want me to be with a family that could take care of me in a way that she couldn't. My parents emphasized that I wasn't different because I was adopted; I was special because I was chosen.

Trying to Measure Up

I feel blessed that every dynamic about my adoption was presented well and in the best possible light. Despite the positivity, however, I still often lived with a sense of fear. Subconsciously, this fear found me seeking to earn my way to stay in my adoptive family. I have three half-siblings from my adoptive father's previous marriage who are significantly older than me. We have great relationships now, but when I was younger, there was some bitterness on their part. They were from a broken home, and now their father was adopting another child who would have an intact family. I began to try to prove to them and others that I belonged in the family. I remember watching during that time a TV drama about a baby who was taken away from her adoptive family. I wondered, "What if that happens to me? What if my birth mother takes me back?" I remember saying to myself, "My parents chose me . . . but what if they choose to give me back?" It was as if I thought my adoption was probationary as long as I was good enough to make them want to keep me.

So what did I do? On my adoptive father's side of the family, the men all went to University of California schools, became Presbyterian elders, joined the army, and had careers in the field of engineering. So I followed in their footsteps. I was ordained as a Presbyterian elder at age 17; attended my dad's alma mater, the University of California, Santa Barbara (although I applied to the United States Military Academy at West Point); became an electrical engineering major; and served in the Reserve Officers Training Core for the first two years of college. All of the things I was involved in were great things. I was a relatively model child, but my fundamental mode of operation was living to gain acceptance, rather than living out of the acceptance I already had.

The mindset of trying to earn my way into the family flowed over into my understanding of my relationship to God. I knew I was saved by grace, but I also thought I needed to measure up. Even into the first ten years of my work in ministry, there was this deep-seated thought that I was performing for God so that he would say, "Well done, good and faithful servant" (Matt. 25:21). I wasn't living out of joy, knowing that I am already accepted in Christ and that nothing I do can make me more or less a part of his kingdom.

I'm not the only one, either. Many believers tend to live out their adoption in Christ the same way I was living out my adoption in my family. They think Christ provisionally accepts them, or that they only have entry level status with him and need to earn their way further in. Their goal now is one of three things: be good enough to stay accepted, earn their way up the Christian ladder, or be in competition with their brothers and sisters in Christ to see who is more a part of the family of God.

Motivated by Delight or Duty?

Paul says at the beginning of Galatians 4 that Jesus was sent into the world so that we would be adopted as children. We are no longer slaves but children of God. Sometimes we can be slaves to a performance-based mode of operation. On the outside, we may look like a great model of Christianity, but our internal motivation can come from a spirit of slavery rather than a spirit of adoption.

To put it another way, two people who sit next to each other in church can both come to church every Sunday, give 10 percent of their income, serve in the ministries of the church, and attend a Bible study. One may be doing all of those things out of the joy of being connected with his or her Father in heaven. The other, however, may being doing these things as part of a checklist to keep his or her Christian credentials, earn more jewels in a heavenly crown, or perhaps even be prideful and pretend to rise above others who don't do as much.

How do we know if we are operating out of delight or duty? Some of the questions in the reflection section can help us examine our own hearts, but one question to ask ourselves as we live the Christian life is whether we are doing something because we "have to" do it or because we "get to" do it. Sometimes I tell my kids to help me with yard work or chores around the house. Usually, telling them they need to help results in the job eventually getting done, but they do the work out of duty. Other times, the kids see me working on something and ask if they can help. When they offer and are excited about it, the job gets done, usually better, and in such a way that my kids and I have a closer relationship.

Another way to understand your motivation is to ask what purpose you are doing it for. Do you want other people to notice how Christian you are? Do you want recognition from others? Or are you doing it because you know deep within that God already loves and accepts you in the same way he loves and accepts Jesus?

Counting the Cost

There is an opposite misunderstanding of our adoption as well—namely, that we use our freedom and acceptance as a way to continue in sin. If we think we can't be any more or less accepted by God than we are now, then why not do what we want and just follow God when it is convenient? Why not turn into spoiled children? That mindset is also a misapplication of the gospel if we assume that all Jesus wants to do is free us and send us on our way.

Being adopted is different than, for example, being a sponsor child. Our family has a sponsor child through a large mission agency that sponsors children throughout the world. We give the required amount and a little extra for Christmas and birthday presents. We write letters from time to time and pray for the child on occasion. I am glad she has a better life than she would without us. I am glad she is hearing about Jesus. I don't, however, agonize over how to make sure she turns out well. She is not written into my will, and I don't wait by the mailbox hoping for a letter or a phone call from her. I have a very different relationship with her as our sponsor child than my parents have with me as their adopted child.

If we think our adoption is that God has made us a sponsor child with limited interaction and a hope for the best, then we don't understand the cost to the Father and the relationship he desires to have with us. He wants us to delight in him. Our life of obedience flows out of our authentic relationship with our God.

When we apply the gospel to our lives, it results not in a sterile following of the rules; nor does it lead to following patterns that are indicative of the world. Applying the gospel results in a loving, intimate relationship, birthed from a deep heart conviction of the truth that the Son of God, who had everything, became nothing in Jesus so that we could become everything to him.

Every Situation and Circumstance

We are called to apply that gospel truth into every aspect of our lives. In Galatians 2:11-14, Paul confronts Peter for perpetuating racism by influencing Jews to withdraw from Gentile Christians. Paul says that not only was the conduct wrong; it was out of step with the truth of the gospel. The truth of the gospel is that Jesus gave up everything in order to associate intimately with us so that we could be associated with him. The truth of the gospel is that when we are adopted in Christ as children of God, we are brothers and sisters with everyone else who believes.

The point of the studies in this section of the book is to help us see that the gospel can be applied to every situation and circumstance in our lives. For example, if I find myself full of worry (even if I have legitimate concerns), do I truly know the depth of God's love that motivated Jesus to go to the cross and secure our position as adopted children, and that nothing can separate me from the love of God in Christ Jesus (Rom. 8:38-39)? If I am trying to find comfort and satisfaction in material needs and other things, perhaps I need to apply the truth that my heavenly Father knows what I need (Matt. 6:32). If in my heart I have experienced the forgiveness of Jesus, how does that lead me to forgive others through the grace of God's forgiving me? Ultimately we can see that every thought, feeling, and action can be shaped by the dynamics of the gospel.

It isn't easy to apply the wonderful truth of our adoption in Christ to our lives. As has been pointed out in previous sessions, to apply the truth of the gospel, we need to do more than know this truth; we need to experience it. In the next session we will delve deeper into what it means to experience the gospel.

Study and Reflection

1. In what ways have you viewed your faith in Jesus as a set of rules that you had to live up to? In what way has the feeling of earning your salvation led to a spirit of competition with other Christians?

2. In what ways have you viewed salvation in Jesus as a license to live or continue to live by the patterns of the world?

3. Read Galatians 2:11-14, where Paul opposes Peter (Cephas), saying that he is not living in step with the gospel. What has Peter been doing here? And why are his actions out of step with the gospel? If Peter were approaching this situation with gospel dynamics, how would he function differently?

4. If Paul were in our church now, how might he say we as a church are living out of step with the gospel?

5. If Paul were talking to you, how might he say you were living out of step with the gospel? In other words, in what ways are you tempted to live out of step with the gospel? What aspects of the gospel might you need to apply more deeply in your life? Are there particular passages of Scripture that you can preach to yourself?

6. As you engage in forming a missional community, how does the gospel influence the way you interact with each other? How will it be both easy and difficult to allow the gospel to shape your interactions with each other? How can you make sure the gospel is appropriately applied to the formation of your group so that you don't move into legalism or a permissive attitude?

7. How does an understanding that you are adopted in Christ increase your intimacy with the Father as opposed to just being saved by the work of Christ? How can you let this reality penetrate your heart in a deeper way and shape your life further?

8. Where do you need to apply the gospel more intentionally in your life? How might you go about doing that?

Prayer

Pray that God by his grace will reveal the depth of the gospel in your life and allow you and your group to apply it to your lives.

Application

During the coming week, develop a rhythm of taking the opportunity three or four times a day to allow God to speak to you in order to reveal where you can apply the gospel in your life.

Session 8

EXPERIENCING THE GOSPEL

BY DAVID HANCOCK

We all, with unveiled face, beholding the glory of the Lord, are being transformed into the same image from one degree of glory to another. For this comes from the Lord who is the Spirit. . . . And even if our gospel is veiled, it is veiled to those who are perishing. In their case the god of this world has blinded the minds of the unbelievers, to keep them from seeing the light of the gospel of the glory of Christ, who is the image of God. For what we proclaim is not ourselves, but Jesus Christ as Lord, with ourselves as your servants for Jesus' sake. For God, who said, "Let light shine out of darkness," has shone in our hearts to give the light of the knowledge of the glory of God in the face of Jesus Christ.

—2 Corinthians 3:18; 4:3–6

What Does It Mean to Experience the Gospel?

Think of yourself as a living, breathing mirror. You, the living mirror, are on one side of a wall, and Christ is on the other side. As you hear the gospel, a window opens in the wall, and you are able to gaze into the face of your Savior (2 Cor. 4:4). And as a mirror, when you gaze on his face, you are transformed to look more and more like him (2 Cor. 3:18; 4:6). This is what it means to experience the gospel.

Experiencing the gospel is when our knowing the gospel in our mind overflows into our entire being. This is when God moves from being a concept or an idea to being very real to us. It's when truth about God leads to intimacy with God. It's when our intellectual understanding of God's love moves to an intimate experience of God's love. We experience the gospel when truth bubbles up into worship. It's like making an outburst because you can't contain the gospel truth any longer. The truth of God's love turns into an experience of being lavished in his love.

Think of our hearts as a geyser. As the truth of who Jesus is and what he did is packed into our hearts, eventually our hearts can't contain the pressure, so they erupt in worship. This is what happens when we look on the face of our Savior. We can't help but praise, worship, glorify, love, follow, and adore him. When we see the face of our Savior, who came into the world to die for us, what else can we do but bow down and worship him?

As Jonathan Edwards said, "There is a difference between having an opinion that God is holy and gracious, and having a sense of the loveliness and beauty of that holiness and grace. There is a difference between having a rational judgment that honey is sweet, and having a sense of its sweetness" (Harold P. Simonson, *Selected Writings of Jonathan Edwards,* 2nd ed., p. 55). We can know that honey is sweet intellectually, but it's not until we taste the honey that we really experience it. The same is true with Christ. We can know the gospel, but it's not until the Holy Spirit allows us to see the face of our Savior that we actually experience the good news of Jesus Christ.

When you experience the gospel, you go from knowing about the gospel intellectually to knowing God personally. Instead of merely reading about God's love in Christ, you are actually lavished by his love. Instead of just studying about Jesus, you start loving him. Some people can be part of a church for decades and know all the truths about Christ but never actually experience his love. So how do we actually experience the gospel? Well, *it is completely by the work of the Holy Spirit.* However, there are some things we can know and do that the Holy Spirit will work through.

How Do We Actually Experience God?

First, we have to understand the depth of our sin, and, *second, we have to understand the depth of God's costly love in Jesus Christ.* Understanding sin and understanding God's costly love produces in us an internal movement created by the Holy Spirit toward experiencing God and the beauty of the gospel.

First, to experience the good news of Jesus Christ, we have to be completely honest with ourselves about the depth of our sin. We have to be willing to lay it all out on the table and feel the weight of it all.

Second, we have to remember who Jesus is and what he did for us. We have to see that as the perfect Son of God he sacrificially stood in our place. He was crushed under the wrath of his Father for our sin, and through faith in Jesus as Savior we receive infinite love and acceptance. As we begin to process all that Christ has done for us, it moves us to experience him through the work of the Holy Spirit.

We begin to experience the gospel when sin and salvation move from concept to reality, from ambiguous to specific, from distant to close. This is not about a forced experience; it is about the work of the Holy Spirit moving us as we are centered in and on the truth of Jesus Christ. While the Holy Spirit does the work, we cooperate with him to bring us face to face with our Savior by centering ourselves in the gospel. Basically what we are doing is understanding both the bad news and the good news.

Knowing the bad news makes the good news sweeter. This is why it is so important that we know the truth of the gospel. We have to understand both the riches of God's love and the depth of our rebellion. From there we turn to Christ as the Savior we rely on. It is a simultaneous turning from sin because we are turning to trust in and rely on Christ. This is our daily repentance.

I would encourage you to look back to the "Knowing the Gospel" session in this book to review the section about sin, being completely honest with yourself and God about your sin. Then I would suggest you review the section about knowing the gospel (specifically with regard to Jesus' incarnation, cross, resurrection, ascension, and return) and try to discover or rediscover God's grace for you in Christ.

How Do We Create Space to Experience God?

Experiencing the gospel is not a one-time event but part of our everyday life. It's about discovering and rediscovering the face of Jesus Christ by looking through the window of the gospel. Along with our daily repentance (seeing our sin and turning to the grace of our Savior), there are spiritual rhythms we can do daily and weekly to create space to experience God. These rhythms are not meant to earn God's love and acceptance but to remind us to center in on the love and acceptance we already have in Christ. Here are a few daily or weekly rhythms that can help us:

- *Reading God's Word:* There is no better place to go than to God's Word in order to explore, discover, and rediscover the good news of Jesus Christ. When reading God's Word, we have to remember that it is not primarily an instruction manual for our life but God's Word to us about how he is saving us. It's God's story about saving us. We must keep that in mind as we explore, discover, and rediscover the riches of God's grace in Christ. All of Scripture points us to Jesus. The Bible is the cord that leads us to our Savior.

- *Preaching the gospel to ourselves:* This is probably one of the most important spiritual disciplines we can have, and it might be foreign to many of us. Do you realize that you preach to yourself more than anyone else does? You are telling yourself something every day about yourself, the world, and God. But what are you preaching to yourself? Are you declaring the good news of who Jesus is and what he did, or something else? I recently asked a group of people to try preaching the gospel to each other at their tables. The room was pretty quiet. Then I asked them to talk about some of the lies they have believed about themselves. The room got pretty loud. We are a lot better at talking about the bad news in our life than telling ourselves the good news of the gospel. Preaching the gospel to yourself is about taking hold of the love and acceptance you have in Christ and learning to live all of your life in response to it. When we preach the gospel to ourselves, we look at all the promises of God and remind ourselves of them every day. We pack them deep down within our hearts over and over and over again so that we might grow in believing them and in reorienting our life around them.

- *Prayer:* The first line of the "Lord's Prayer" found in Matthew 6:9-13 addresses "Our Father in heaven." The start of this prayer tells us we have access to the King of heaven like a child has access to his father. Prayer is about having intimacy with our Father, who is the King of heaven. It's about crawling up into the lap of the King of creation and calling him Father. This is only available to us through Christ. Jesus brought us into a relationship with the Father through all that he did for us. This is something we ought to reflect on every time we are in prayer. Also, in prayer we are creating space so that we might confess our sins to the Father and then see how all those sins have been forgiven in Christ. Prayer should always take us right to the gospel.

- *Corporate worship:* In corporate worship sinners are able to gather together to hear the gospel preached to them, sing of the gospel, and pray through the gospel. Many people today see Sunday morning worship as irrelevant for their lives. But if the gospel is being preached, sung, and prayed to sinners and by sinners, it should be one of the most encouraging parts of our week.

- *Community:* This is about having a group of people whom you can trust as you confess your sins and who can point you to the truth and promises of the gospel. They are people who encourage you in the gospel so that you may live life fully alive in Christ. It's not a group that encourages you through positive thinking or tells you to try harder. It's a group of people who are helping each other live in step with the truth of the gospel.

- *Sabbath rest:* In our busy, make-it-happen culture we have to ask ourselves, "Do we trust God enough to rest?" Should we work hard? Of course, but we should also rest, reminding ourselves that we have a God who is in control of all things and is taking care of us. Unless the Lord is doing the work, all of our labor is in vain (Ps. 127:1).

Summary

In order to behold the face of our Savior, we have to create space in our lives for the gospel to permeate. And as we experience the gospel, we behold Christ and are transformed from the inside out from one degree of glory to another. This means we are changed to become more like Christ. It means that as we behold Christ, we become more like him. We are like mirrors. And as we behold Christ, we are transformed more and more into his image (2 Cor. 3:18).

Experiencing the good news of Jesus Christ and seeing him face to face gives us power to live differently. Think about it like this: You can't really forgive unless you have experienced being forgiven by God. You can't really love unless you have experienced God's love for you. You can't have mercy on others unless you have experienced God's mercy toward you. You can't serve unless you have experienced how Jesus has already served you. The power to live differently comes from experiencing the gospel of Jesus Christ by the work of the Holy Spirit.

Study and Reflection

1. Have you been experiencing God in profound ways lately? If so, explain.

2. According to this session, what are the two things we must understand in order to experience God? How honest are you being with yourself and God about your sin? How honest are you being with yourself about God's grace? Have you come to understand the depth of your sin and the depth of God's love for you?

3. The better you know the truth of the gospel, the better you are able to experience the gospel. What are some actions you can take to better learn the gospel?

4. Have you been creating space to experience God through daily and weekly rhythms?

5. "These rhythms are not meant to earn God's love and acceptance but to remind us to center in on the love and acceptance we already have in Christ." In what ways have you used these rhythms or disciplines to try to earn God's love and acceptance? What can help you use them the way they are intended?

6. How can you help each other in your daily and weekly rhythms?

Prayer

This week, pray that the Holy Spirit will help you experience God as you reflect on the gospel of Jesus Christ.

Application

This week, be intentional about creating space to experience God through spiritual rhythms.

Session 9

SPEAKING THE GOSPEL TO ONE ANOTHER

BY DANA ALLIN

An Ongoing Process

We often assume a false dichotomy between evangelism and discipleship. We assume that in evangelism we share the gospel so that people who don't believe in Jesus will believe in him and become Christians. But after they believe, we assume they no longer need to be evangelized; now they just need to know theological truths and understand lists of behavioral and attitudinal expectations that they need to follow so that they can be the kind of people God wants them to be. The assumption is that as these individuals conform to behavioral and attitudinal expectations, they will be growing as more mature disciples. Certainly the Lord wants us to conform to Christ, but the real question is, How do people conform to the gospel? Do people conform their lives by knowing a list of requirements? The answer is no! We see all throughout the Old Testament that simply giving lists of rights and wrongs doesn't change a person. Even if those individuals end up conforming to those behaviors on the outside, their hearts are not transformed. Jesus in Matthew 23 gives a series of warnings to the Pharisees that while their outside behavior may conform to a set of behavior lists, they are still not in a right relationship with God because their hearts are not right.

Behaviors actually stem from the underlying beliefs, attitudes, and values of a person or group. What Jesus ultimately wants to see changed in people's lives is not just their outward behavior but more importantly their internal beliefs, attitudes, and values. This change occurs when the exact same gospel that is spoken to lead to initial conversion is continually spoken after conversion. The gospel ("good news") is continually spoken throughout the discipleship process to continually bring about conversion in the image of Christ.

I first understood this reality during my initial year as pastor of Indian River Presbyterian Church. We had been making some important and much-needed changes, and of course we were experiencing some discontentment because of those changes. I was taking much of the pushback personally, to the point where it was affecting the core understanding of who I was. As I began processing this issue with some other friends in ministry, I was challenged with a question about whether I believed in the gospel. I was frankly a little appalled: "Of course I believe in the gospel; I am an evangelical minister of the gospel." The reality, however, was that in this particular situation my identity was wrapped up in my performance and what people thought of me rather than in the performance of Jesus Christ and what he thought of me.

This helped me realize that even though I am already a Christian, in order for me to grow as a Christian I need to continue to have people speak the good news of the gospel in my life so that I can continually be rooted in him.

It can be challenging to actually speak the gospel to our fellow brothers and sisters in Christ. In this session we will look at some of the principles involved in speaking the gospel to one another in love.

Principle 1: Examine Yourself Before Speaking the Gospel to One Another

In Matthew 7:1-5, Jesus says that in our interactions with one another we need to take the log out of our own eye before we help someone take the speck of sawdust out of their eye. Notice that the passage doesn't say we shouldn't help someone take the speck out of their eye, but to do so, we must see if there are any logs in our own eyes.

This process of self-examination involves several steps. First, we need to check our *motivation* for speaking the gospel to someone. Do we, for example, like the fact that the speck in someone else's eye makes us feel superior to them? There are times when we might want to "speak the truth" to someone not out of love for them but to satisfy our own egotistical impulse.

Second, we need to check our own *adequacy* in hearing and applying the gospel. My job includes a fair amount of air travel, so I often hear flight attendants giving instructions about what would happen in the unlikely event of a loss of cabin pressure. We are told that if the oxygen masks drop, we should first put on our own masks and then assist others who may need help with theirs. This principle holds true for speaking the gospel to one another. We need to first breathe in the air of the gospel before we try to assist others in applying the dynamics of the gospel to their lives. Before we help others, we need to make sure we are continually saturated in the gospel by hearing it ourselves.

Principle 2: Speak the Gospel, Not the Application of the Gospel

When someone we care about is not living a gospel-saturated life, the temptation is to jump into telling them how they need to change their attitude or behavior in light of the gospel of Jesus. That may come later, but it is not the first step. For example, if someone is holding on to a grudge and not forgiving others, our temptation will be to say, "Jesus forgave you for so much, so you ought to forgive others." While this is completely true, we shouldn't make that jump for them. In previous sessions we noted that knowing the gospel involves more than simply understanding and agreeing with the facts of the gospel; it also means experiencing the gospel. In this case, it means experiencing God's forgiveness ourselves. Only when we experience the gospel can we apply the gospel. Our job, then, is to prayerfully speak the core of the gospel to people and allow the Spirit of God to help them experience (or experience again) the truth of the gospel so that they can apply God's good news to their situation.

The following examples can help to illustrate speaking the gospel to one another.

Example 1: Gospel Motivation

One man in our community was a teacher in an elementary school and was considering a change of career by going into ordained ministry. On the surface this idea seemed great! We always want quality men and women to pursue ministry as a career. However, in talking with him about his situation, there seemed to be two motivations that were out of sync with the gospel. First, it appeared that he felt that his current career was less important than a career in ministry might be. Second, he liked leading Bible study, but it often seemed that he mostly enjoyed having knowledge that other people didn't, which made him feel a little superior to them. Both of these attitudes seemed out of sync with the gospel. Whether or not he was called into full-time ministry, these two issues needed to be dealt with.

It would have been easy for us, having seen these two things, to point them out and tell him that his identity should be based on who he is in Jesus and not what he does. He would have probably acknowledged this in mind, but that acknowledgement alone probably wouldn't have changed his attitude. Instead, the community asked questions about why he wanted to make this change. When the hints came up where his attitude was not consistent with the gospel, the group then had to ask (not tell!) him, "What is your position in Christ?" He knew the answer, but he needed to verbalize his identity in the gospel of Jesus Christ. The group needed to reinforce his identity in Christ and use various Scriptures to help reinforce his appropriation of the gospel at a deeper level. Once the reality of his position in Christ had sunk in at a deeper level, he began to see where his motivations were flawed and needed to be altered. After reorienting his motivations, he was able to determine whether he was truly called to professional ministry by Christ, rather than by his distorted thinking.

Example 2: Substitute Loves

A young woman was bouncing from relationship to relationship. It was clear that she felt she needed to be in a relationship in order to feel complete. Her friends had recognized this in her for years and would lovingly explain their perceptions. She often brushed them off or minimized their concerns. However, once she got involved in a missional community in which people were speaking the truth of the gospel to each other, this truth started to sink in at a deeper level. She recognized that she was substituting the fleeting love and affection of men for the steadfast love of Jesus. She ended up devoting more time to understanding her relationship with Jesus. When she did finally get back into a dating relationship, it was much healthier because it came out of her relationship with Jesus and didn't replace the love she had for Jesus.

Speaking the gospel to one another takes grace, patience, and love. However, when we commit to doing this with one another, there will be lasting transformation.

Reflection and Discussion

1. When has someone spoken the truth in love to you? When have you had to do that for someone else?

2. What is the difference between saying something difficult to someone in a loving way and actually speaking the gospel to someone?

3. Read John 4:1-26, 39-42, which tells of Jesus' interacting with the Samaritan woman at the well. How does Jesus speak the gospel to her? In comparison to being told not to do something, how does hearing the gospel motivate her to change her behavior?

4. Can you think of examples in which you sensed you should advise someone about their behavior or attitude and yet needed to examine yourself first? In the future, how can you make sure you have examined yourself before speaking the gospel to others?

5. When have you been open to letting others speak the gospel to you? When have you not been so open? How can you make sure you are open to hearing the gospel?

6. When have you spoken the gospel to yourself, or when might you have spoken the gospel to yourself rather than ignoring an opportunity to do so or scolding yourself for certain behaviors or attitudes?

7. Think about the following situations. How would you speak the gospel to these individuals?
   - Someone who isn't giving of their resources to a ministry because they are afraid they won't have enough left over. Or perhaps they don't give because they would rather enjoy material possessions or travel or recreational experiences.
   - Someone who is sarcastic toward others or acts as if they are better than others.
   - Someone who has a habit of putting himself or herself down.

Prayer

Ask God for wisdom in knowing when and how to steer difficult conversations toward speaking the gospel to one another.

Application

During the coming week consider doing the following:

- Identify areas in your daily life in which your attitudes or actions are out of step with the gospel, and speak the gospel to your particular situation.
- Try to find gentle ways to speak the truth of the gospel into the lives of other members of your group.

COMMUNITY

Session 10

HOW THE GOSPEL FORMS COMMUNITY

BY DAVID HANCOCK

In the previous section we considered what it means to believe the gospel. In this section we look at how the gospel affects community, and in this opening session about community we see how the gospel forms true community.

Community and Commitment

Romans 15:7 tells us, "Welcome one another as Christ has welcomed you, for the glory of God." What does Paul, the writer of Romans, mean here by "welcome"—or, as other translations say, "accept" or "receive"? The word in the original Greek text, from the root word *proslambano,* means "to grasp, take hold of, and pull in." Here we are given a picture of Christ grasping us with his hands, taking hold of us, and pulling us in. Jesus pulls us in close and speaks gently but powerfully: "I will never leave you or forsake you. I am yours and you are mine forever."

When we become Christians, God makes a covenant, or promise, with us that he will be our God and we will be his people. We have been saved to be in relationship with him. This covenant also brings us into relationship with God's people. This is the formation of Christian community. As a result of God's commitment to us, we are joined to him and to the rest of his people. Christian community is a *community of commitment*. Christ's commitment to us produces in us a commitment to him and to the community he is forming. What we are being told, then, is to grasp, take hold of, and pull each other in as Christ has grasped, taken hold of, and pulled us in. What we see here is covenant community, a community of commitment.

What does it look like to be a community of people committed to each other? A community of commitment has several characteristics. It is

- a community that is together often.
- a community of people who trust each other.
- a community immersed in the gospel together.

A Community That Is Together Often

A community of commitment is a group of people who are together often enough to express their commitment to each other. That means spending less time doing other things individually. So it probably is not surprising that every group with whom I have taken this study has shown the most push-back when we have begun focusing on community commitment. After all, we are all busy. One group resisted because many of its members were in the middle of attaining master's degrees and had no time. Another group had a lot of young children and no time. A third group consisted of middle-aged parents who, on a typical weekday, had to bring one child to soccer practice and pick up another from tennis while in the meantime tending to the ongoing care of ailing parents. But a true community can often help one another in such things. We like the idea of community, but the sacrifices that come with commitment to a community can be challenging. Even so, those sacrifices are worthwhile.

Why? Because we are all wired for community. We are made in the image of God, and God exists in perfect community. Some people have thought that God created the world because he was lonely, but that is not the case. Creation is an overflow of God's life in perfect community.

In contrast, we live in a very individualistic society. For example, look at the way our homes are designed. For many of us, we drive up to our residence and into our garage, and often we can step right into our homes with our fenced-in backyards without ever seeing our neighbors. The media have also realized that we are starving for community, so they create programming like *Modern Family, The Office*, and "reality" TV. Notice what the characters of these shows do. They stop what they are doing, look directly into the camera, and have a conversation with you. Your community has just become these people on TV.

Sacrifice is required in order to have community; however, it is worthwhile. When it comes to the community that God is building, each one of us needs to ask, "Am I willing to make the necessary sacrifices to be part of this community?" To answer this question, we may need to wrestle with another one: "Am I more concerned about what I want to do, or about the community of people that Jesus is forming and wants me to be a part of?"

A Community of People Who Trust Each Other

Commitment produces trust. We trust God because there is nothing we can do or not do that will cause God to love us more or less. God is committed to loving us because he credits Christ's record to us. We are his, and he is ours. The same ought to be true of Christian community. We should be able to say to each other, "There is nothing you can do or not do that will cause me to love you more or less." The Father accepts us the way we are through faith in Christ, and that is how we need to accept one another. This unconditional acceptance produces trust.

But it doesn't end there. We may be accepted as we are through Christ, but God loves us so much that he empowers us in Christ to change more and more into who he created us to be. The same ought to be true of Christian community—that we accept each other as we are, but we love each other enough to encourage each other to become more and more of who God created us to be. If we are truly committed to one another, we will encourage each other to grow into the people, in Christ, whom God has made us to be (see 2 Cor. 3:18). The process goes like this, through the ongoing work of God's Spirit in us:

- When we trust each other, we can be honest with each other.
- When we can be honest, we can confess our sins.
- When we can confess our sins, others can encourage us in the gospel.
- When this happens, we are in an ideal environment for growth.

Let me explain this a little further. In his book *You Can Change,* Tim Chester says, "Sin is like mold: it grows best in the dark. Expose it to the light, and it starts to dry up." He later explains that if we aren't confessing our sins to others, our reputation matters more to us than our holiness. When we confess our sins to each other, our sins are brought into the light. Then the community encourages us to be changed by speaking the truth of the gospel to us. Our growth is a communal effort rather than an individualistic effort. We have been wired to grow together by knowing, applying, experiencing, and speaking the gospel together in community. And trust is a vital part of this process.

Do you trust the people in your community? Do you accept everyone in your community? Are you willing to walk with them as they are growing? Living this way doesn't happen by our own effort; it is linked into Christ's commitment to us. That brings us to the question "Where do we get the power to live like this?" We receive this power from Christ by his Spirit, through becoming a community of people immersed in the truth of the gospel together.

A Community Immersed in the Gospel Together

The power to live as a community of people committed to God and each other can come only from knowing, applying, and experiencing God's commitment to us in the gospel.

We must together be grafted into Christ. In John 15:5 Jesus says, "I am the vine; you are the branches." Jesus is primarily telling us that he is the source of our growth, but he is also revealing that he is the link to the other branches. Only through him can we truly know others and be known by them. He gives us unity through his commitment to us.

If we are having problems committing to each other, we need a radical reorientation to Christ's commitment to us. This happens only through a growing relationship with God through the Word and prayer. If you really want to experience being the kind of community we are talking about, you have to be in the Word together. This means not just opening up the Bible, but immersing your lives in Scripture together. To be more specific, this means seeing how Scripture points us to the gospel of Jesus Christ.

The gospel shows that the Father, Son, and Holy Spirit are in a community so perfect that they are one God. They are so committed to each other that they are one. Yet Jesus emptied himself and came to live among us and even die in our place so that he could grasp, take hold of, and pull us in. On the cross he bore the cost of our sin—total separation from God—and gave up his life so that we would not have to pay that cost. He made the ultimate sacrifice for us so that he could welcome us into ultimate community with God.

Through faith in Christ, you and your community are swept up into the community of the triune God. You can stand together, knowing that you are God's community and that he is your God. Grasp, take hold of, and pull each other in as Christ has grasped, taken hold of, and pulled you into his community. It's well worth the sacrifice, by God's power at work in us, to help people come in and grow to enjoy full life in Christ.

Discussion Questions

1. Are you a person who runs from community? Why?

2. Is your community a community of commitment? What may need to change for it to become that kind of community?

3. Why might you or your group push back from spending time together and being committed to each other?

4. What sacrifices will you have to make to become a truly committed covenant community?

5. Is anything scaring you about this conversation? If so, what is it?

6. What are some things you can do together as a community that you have been doing individually?

7. Are you a community of people who trust each other? Why or why not? If not, what needs to change?

8. There is nothing you can do or not do that will cause God to love you more or less. The same should be true of the love of the community of Christ. What challenges do you face individually and as a group to extend God's love in this way?

9. Christian community is about accepting each other the way we are and loving each other enough to encourage change, by the power of Christ. How does this statement make you feel? What can you do to help your community live more like this?

Prayer and Application

Pray daily for one another and for your community as a whole to experience and to show God's sacrificial, abundant love, as taught by Christ in his Word and through his example.

In the coming week, take the time and make the effort to hang out together and enjoy each other's company.

Session 11

HOW THE GOSPEL SHAPES COMMUNITY

BY DAVID HANCOCK

What is essential in the shaping and building up of Christian community? What tears down Christian community?

Love and Humility v. Pride and Conceit

We have seen how the gospel forms true community. Now, with the help of Romans 12:9-21 and Philippians 2:1-11, we look at how the gospel shapes community.

Romans 12:9 says, "Let love be genuine." What is genuine love? In a sermon on this passage, John Piper says that genuine love is love that "forgets itself." In his book *The Freedom of Self-Forgetfulness,* Tim Keller says something very similar about humility: "Gospel humility is not thinking more of myself or less of myself, it is thinking of myself less." When you think about yourself less, you think of others more. The opposite of this is seen in Romans 12:16, which warns against being haughty or prideful or full of conceit. Why does Paul, the writer of Romans, include this warning? Because pride involves excessive desire for oneself. Pride is the opposite of selfless love and humility, making us think of ourselves more and others less. Whereas genuine love and humility praise others, pride and conceit steal praise from others and applaud the self. Love and humility give glory, while pride and conceit steal glory.

We can picture the difference like this: Love means bending down and bringing yourself low in order to put your hands under someone else's feet to hoist them up. Pride, on the other hand, is like climbing a ladder to be higher up than someone else, and then tying a weight around that person's neck to keep them down. Genuine love and humility elevate others, but pride and conceit bring others down.

C. S. Lewis explains in *Mere Christianity* that pride is the root of all sin. Adam and Eve ate the forbidden fruit because, as the devil tempted them to think, they wanted to be like God and steal the glory and praise he deserved. Just as this act destroyed their community with God and with one another, pride does the same to us. When we are prideful and others receive the praise, honor, or glory that we want, we either compete with them or belittle them. Think about a talent that you have, one you are good at and known for being good at. If you find that a peer is also praised for that talent, you may be tempted to compete with or try to downplay his or her talent to bring glory back to yourself. Such cancerous jealousy is caused by pride, and it can tear down and destroy community. Why? Because there can be no unity when we want to bring others down.

There is a story about a woman who sat down to eat with two great leaders on consecutive nights. Both were impressive men; however, the woman left each meal with two completely different impressions. After eating with the first leader, she felt like *he* was the cleverest man in England. But she found that while eating with the second leader, he made her feel like *she* was the cleverest woman in England. When spending time with others, do you concentrate on trying to prove how great you are, or do you try to lift others up? If we stop and think about it, we probably spend more time doing the former than we would like to admit. The problem is, that kind of behavior destroys community and is not shaped by the gospel.

Can you imagine what would happen if a whole community lowered themselves in order to lift others up? What would your community look like if you stopped seeking your own praise and honor and instead sought to elevate everyone else? How can we be people who live with love and humility instead of pride and conceit?

The Gospel of God's Love and Humility

In Philippians 2:1-11, Paul urges us to be a community of people who bring themselves low in order to lift others up, a community of humility and love. The power to live that way comes from Jesus, who first brought himself low so that we might be lifted up. When we recognize that Jesus did that for us, we are given a new identity that compels us to do the same for others. Let's look at this process in more detail by discussing three questions:

- Where do love and humility come from?
- How do we get the desire to be genuinely loving and humble toward others?
- How do we get the desire to genuinely love God and glorify him over ourselves?

Where do love and humility come from? The answer is God; he is the source of love and humility. As 1 John 4:7-8 says, "Let us love one another, for love is from God, and whoever loves has been born of God and knows God. Anyone who does not love does not know God, because God is love." Think about this: if God is the only source of love, then God must be more than one person. Why? Because genuine love and humility are selfless. Therefore genuine love originates in the Trinity as the persons of God—Father, Son, and Holy Spirit—are continually lifting each other up. Instead of fighting to keep their own praise, glory and honor, each works for the praise, glory, and honor of the others. The Trinity is a perfect picture of genuine love and humility.

Because our creator loves this way, we too, being made in his image, are called to love this way.

How do we get the desire to be genuinely loving and humble toward others? The answer is that we receive and are filled with God's love, which then overflows from us to others. God is the only source of genuine love, so our love for others must come from God.

Blaise Pascal wrote in his great work, *Pensées,* that there is an abyss (or huge space) within each of us that is meant to be filled by God. When God fills that gaping space, we have the ability to love because God, the source of love, is within us fueling us to love. But if we try to fill that space with anything other than God, we don't have access to the true source of love. St. Augustine said that if we fill this hole with anything other than God, it is a "disordered love." Disordered loves prevent us from truly loving others. However, if God is filling the gap within us, then we have the capacity to love, because God, who is love, is living within us.

C. S. Lewis builds on this idea, teaching that there are first things and second things. First things are God and his Word, and second things are all that God has created. If you make first things first and second things second, you enjoy both; but if you make second things first, you enjoy neither.

In other words, *we can't genuinely love if God is not our first love.* I have seen my capacity to love others grow as my love for God has grown. In the same way, becoming a genuinely loving community starts with loving God. If you are having problems loving others, you need to take an honest look at your love for God.

How do we get the desire to genuinely love God? The answer, again, is in 1 John 4 and Philippians 2. In 1 John 4:19 we read, "We love because he first loved us." So if we want to love God more, we have to comprehend the extent to which he loves us.

Let's look at God's love for us, displayed in sending his Son to save us and in Jesus' willing self-sacrifice for our sake. Philippians 2:5-8 beautifully describes this: "Christ Jesus . . . though he was in the form of God, did not count equality with God a thing to be grasped, but emptied himself, by taking the form of a servant, being born in the likeness of men. And being found in human form, he humbled himself by becoming obedient to the point of death, even death on a cross."

The perfect picture of genuine love is the grace and humility of our God, who lowered himself to the point of death on a cross in order to lift us up. Our Savior was in a perfect, selfless relationship in heavenly glory, yet he left that to be humbled and crushed on a cross for our sake. As God says in Deuteronomy 32:35, "Vengeance is mine" (see Rom. 12:19), but instead of dealing out punishment, Christ came to absorb the vengeance earned by our sinful pride. Because Jesus did this for you and for me, we are now able to enter into loving community with him.

Our deeply sinful pride was crushed on the cross by a perfectly selfless love that stirs us to humility. Our humble and loving Savior overcomes evil by rising from the dead, and now, through our union with Christ, we are lifted up into loving community with the holy Trinity. Together we stand as a community with our God! How could we then for any reason not give him praise and sing of his glory? In summary, if you want to love others, love God. If you want to love God, you must see the great love he has for you and your community. And now, as a community immersed in the love of God for us, we cannot live without showing love and humility toward one another. Why? Because we have received undeserving love in the humility of Christ.

Discussion Questions

1. Genuine love and humility involve not thinking more of oneself or less of oneself but thinking of oneself less. How would our thoughts and actions change if we lived more like this every day?

2. In what areas of your life do you find yourself competing with or belittling others? Why? What can you do instead to bring yourself low in order to lift others up?

3. What are some examples of how pride and conceit have destroyed community?

4. Where do love and humility come from?

5. How do we get the desire to be genuinely loving and humble toward others?

6. How do we get the desire to genuinely love God and glorify him?

Prayer and Application

Keep praying daily that God's love may fill and shape you to be the community he calls you to be.

Look for ways to lower yourself in order to bring glory to God. Think about how it makes you feel. Watch how it brings you closer to God.

Look for ways to lower yourself in order to lift someone else up. Think about how it makes you feel. Think about how it makes the other person feel. Watch how it brings you closer to that person.

Session 12

COMMUNITY: A DISPLAY OF THE GOSPEL

BY DAVID HANCOCK

Reflecting the Gospel

The community I belong to gathers together once a week to study the Bible. We also gather another day of the week to eat together and just hang out and enjoy each other's company. These gatherings outside of Bible study give us an opportunity to invite people who aren't Christians to experience a community that is formed and shaped by the gospel. Recently someone in our community brought an older neighbor to one of our gatherings. He commented that had experienced real love from maybe two people in his life, but when he looked around at the people at this gathering, he could see that they *all* had this kind of love for each other. He said he had never seen anything like it. What was he seeing? The effects of the gospel displayed in a covenant community.

The gospel produces a community of people who display commitment, love, humility, and the fruit of the gospel. This community is made up not of people who have it all together, but of people who can love and forgive in the midst of life's messiness. It's not a community without problems, but it is one that stays committed to each other through the problems it faces. It's a community of people who love because they are loved though Christ, who forgive because they have been forgiven, and who accept because they know deep acceptance from God. Christian community displays the gospel because it is filled with people who are experiencing the gospel and reflecting it.

How exactly do we display the gospel? Jesus put it this way in Matthew 5:13-16:

> "You are the salt of the earth, but if salt has lost its taste, how shall its saltiness be restored? It is no longer good for anything except to be thrown out and trampled under people's feet.
>
> "You are the light of the world. A city set on a hill cannot be hidden. Nor do people light a lamp and put it under a basket, but on a stand, and it gives light to all in the house. In the same way, let your light shine before others, so that they may see your good works and give glory to your Father who is in heaven."

Let's look at these two metaphors in more detail as ways in which we display the gospel.

Salt

Jesus tells us we are "the salt of the earth." Salt (sodium chloride) is necessary for survival and also prevents decay. It acts as a preservative, which is why sailors used to bring salted meat with them on long voyages. What Jesus is telling us is that when we become a community shaped by the gospel, we go into the lives of the people around us and reverse the effects of decay in their lives.

Your community is called to be a preservative in your city. It's called to be a community that comes to the aid of broken and hurting people around you. When you say yes to Jesus, you say yes to being a community of people who work toward the renewal of your neighbors, coworkers, friends, and family.

We see from Rodney Stark's book *The Rise of Christianity* how the early church was the salt of the earth:

> "Christianity served as a revitalization movement that arose in response to the misery, chaos, fear, and brutality of life in the urban Greco-Roman world. . . . Christianity revitalized life in Greco-Roman cities by providing new norms and new kinds of social relationships able to cope with many urgent problems. To cities filled with the homeless and impoverished, Christianity offered charity as well as hope. To cities filled with newcomers and strangers, Christianity offered an immediate basis for attachment. To cities filled with orphans and widows, Christianity provided a new and expanded sense of family. To cities torn by violent ethnic strife, Christianity offered a new basis for social solidarity. And to cities faced with epidemics, fire, and earthquakes, Christianity offered effective nursing services. . . . For what they brought was not simply an urban movement, but a new culture capable of making life in Greco-Roman cities more tolerable."

Later in his book Stark explains that because Christians lived this way, others became Christians because they saw a love that was truly giving and a joy that was able to rise up even in the midst of despair. This glimpse of what life was like with Christ and the riches he offers, stirred people to faith.

How is God calling your community to be like salt in the lives of your neighbors, friends, and coworkers?

Light

Jesus also described the Christian community as "the light of the world." Without light we cannot see. Our world has been darkened by sin and drained of light—so our neighbors and coworkers can't see God clearly; they have a distorted view of God. Christian community can overcome this spiritual blindness by displaying the light of the gospel to the people around them.

We know from the gospel of John that Christ is the true light (John 1:1-13; 8:12), and we bring that light into the world when Christ shines through us. When light shines on something through another object, we call that refraction. We see this in how lenses are used to manipulate light in order to change the size or clarity of what something looks like, as with a magnifying glass or a microscope. As people through whom the light of Christ shines, we have an effect on how the world sees God. What does Jesus look like through your community? Is he easy to see or hard to find? Is he bright or dull? Is he clear or blurred?

The more your community immerses itself in the truth of the gospel, the clearer Christ becomes to those who are looking on. This is not because the community has it all together; it's simply that the community knows the One who does. We must learn to be communities who are looking on the face of our Savior more and more so that we might display the truth of his glory to the world.

If we want the world to see Christ's glory, we can't hide what the gospel produces. Jesus describes Christian community as the corporate image of God, shining like a city on a hill. This means we should be inviting people into our community so that they can see the effects of the gospel. Only then will our friends, family, neighbors, and coworkers start to see what life is like with Jesus, including all the riches he offers us in the gospel.

Communities formed and shaped by the gospel are attractive, and people want to be part of communities like this. People want approval, acceptance, and love; and your Christian community has the ability to be that in Christ. How? By receiving perfect approval, acceptance, and love in and through Christ. We are able to give to others what we have received in Christ. And when we invite friends and neighbors into this community, they see people who have discovered that life has a meaning and purpose beyond simply living for themselves and their own comfort. Here our friends can begin to see that maybe Jesus is worth looking into.

We grow into a full-life community because our Savior is the true salt of the earth and the true light of the world. He has come to reverse the world's decay and to display the light of God's love for us. By coming into the world and dying on the cross, he took on decay and death for our sake. And because he now lives, raised victorious over death, darkness, and decay, we are preserved through faith and now see God through the light of Christ. We are called to be a community that displays the truth that Jesus is the light of the world and the Savior who brings us into relationship with God.

Discussion Questions

1. What stops you from inviting your non-believing friends, neighbors, and coworkers to hang out with your Christian community?

2. What are the common negative stereotypes about Christians that might be true of your community?

3. Think about being "the salt of the earth." What do you think God might be calling your community to do in order to be salt in the lives of your friends, neighbors, and coworkers? What is the next step in helping to make this happen?

4. Think about being "the light of the world." What do you think God might be calling your community to do in order to shine the light of Christ into the lives of your friends, neighbors, and coworkers? What is the next step in helping to make this happen?

5. Do you have opportunities to invite people into your community so that they might be able to see a display of what the gospel produces? If so, how can you be more intentional about displaying the gospel? If not, what could you start doing to make opportunities available?

Prayer and Application

In your prayers each day, ask Jesus to help you find ways and see opportunities to be like salt and light for your friends, neighbors, and coworkers, displaying the full life of the gospel in your personal relationships and in your community.

Assess what people see when they look at your life and your community. Do they see an amazing, life-giving Savior? Do they see people who need a Savior and who have found the joy of full life in him? If not, what changes will you and your community need to make in order to faithfully represent Jesus?

MISSION

Session 13

GO

BY DAVID HANCOCK

Up to this point we have learned what it means to believe the gospel and what happens when a community immerses its life together in the truth of the gospel. Now let's look at how a community can lead others to faith and help them grow in faith. In this opening session on mission we will look at how we are called to make disciples where we live, work, and play. We start by building relationships with the people God has placed around us. And as we go to them, we go with the same posture Christ had in coming to us—sacrificially.

Citizens of Heaven Living on Earth

The apostle Paul encourages believers to see their relationship with God and with others as follows (2 Cor. 5:17–21):

> If anyone is in Christ, he is a new creation. The old has passed away; behold, the new has come. All this is from God, who through Christ reconciled us to himself and gave us the ministry of reconciliation; that is, in Christ God was reconciling the world to himself, not counting their trespasses against them,

> and entrusting to us the message of reconciliation. Therefore, we are ambassadors for Christ, God making his appeal through us. We implore you on behalf of Christ, be reconciled to God. For our sake he made him to be sin who knew no sin, so that in him we might become the righteousness of God.

Notice that we are described as "ambassadors." An ambassador is someone who is officially appointed to represent their home country while living in another country. Paul is explaining that we are ambassadors in the sense that we are citizens of heaven appointed by God to represent heaven to the world while we are living here in the world. Through our service as his ambassadors, God is making his appeal to our friends, neighbors, and coworkers. And what is that appeal? To be reconciled to God. How can people be reconciled? Through Christ, who reconciles us to God and to each other through faith. God calls us to a ministry of reconciliation. As his personal ambassadors, we invite our friends, neighbors, and coworkers to be reconciled with God, to become newly created in Christ, and to enter into the citizenship of heaven. Think of it this way: we are conduits that connect people to Jesus.

Go

Before he ascended to heaven, Jesus came to his followers and announced (Matt. 28:18–20):

> "All authority in heaven and on earth has been given to me. Go therefore and make disciples of all nations, baptizing them in the name of the Father and of the Son and of the Holy Spirit, teaching them to observe all that I have commanded you. And behold, I am with you always, to the end of the age."

Ambassadors are called to go on a mission. In verse 19 the word for "Go" is a passive participle. A better reading would be "as you are going." When we read it this way, "Therefore, as you are going, make disciples . . ." we get a better understanding of what Jesus is telling us. Jesus is saying that wherever you are, be making disciples. By telling us,

"Go," Jesus is not necessarily saying we must go to a different place, like a missionary to a foreign country. While God calls some people to do that, most of us are called to be missionaries where we live, work, and play. In other words, if we have not sensed a call to do mission work in another place, we are probably already where God has called us to be. So we simply need to be intentional about building relationships with the people God has put in our lives. Our neighbors and coworkers are not there by accident. I believe God has put each person in our lives for a reason. Our next step, then, is to start developing relationships with them. And as relationships are being developed, we can lean on Jesus' promise that he is "with [us] always" (Matt. 28:20). What's more, because "all authority in heaven and on earth has been given" to him (28:18), he will work things out exactly as he has planned.

Therefore, as ambassadors, we are simply called to be faithful in what God has called us to do in everyday life, and the Holy Spirit works out the rest. Take comfort that he is with you and in control of what happens. I have been friends with people for years who are not ready to come to any type of Bible study or corporate worship. Other friends have jumped right into the church. Either way, Jesus is with us in our work as his ambassadors, and he is in control. Our goal is to be faithful in inviting people into a community immersed in the gospel that can guide them to faith. Sometimes their coming to faith can be a long process, and sometimes it can be quick. In some cases, sadly, it might never happen. But that's not up to us; it's up to God. He is sovereign over all things. Our role is to be faithful in bringing people into environments where they can hear and understand the gospel and be shown what it means to be a Christian.

Now, what is our posture when we are building these relationships? How exactly do we go? We go incarnationally in two ways: by immersion and by sacrifice.

Immerse

When we look at the incarnation of Christ, we see that Jesus first comes to us, becoming fully human like us while remaining fully God. In following Christ, we go into the world, as citizens of heaven living on earth, yet we remain citizens of heaven. We become like our friends, yet we remain distinct from them. We do not join in the sinful behavior of this world, but as ambassadors of God we bring Christ into the world, representing him faithfully as the Savior who has made it possible for us to be reconciled with God. We get into the world while remaining distinct so that we can best know how our friends, neighbors, and coworkers need to hear the gospel.

This is the way Paul lived. In 1 Corinthians 9:19-23 Paul tells us,

> Though I am free from all, I have made myself a servant to all, that I might win more of them. To the Jews I became as a Jew, in order to win Jews. To those under the law I became as one under the law (though not being myself under the law) that I might win those under the law. To those outside the law I became as one outside the law (not being outside the law of God but under the law of Christ) that I might win those outside the law. To the weak I became weak, that I might win the weak. I have become all things to all people, that by all means I might save some. I do it all for the sake of the gospel, that I may share with them in its blessings.

Paul immersed himself in the lives of the people around him so that they might know the truth of Christ. He fit into their culture and became like them while remaining a faithful follower of Christ. We are to do the same.

This means we need to immerse ourselves into the lives of those around us. Getting to know them and be known by them, we will see how and where they need Jesus most in their life. This means more than just a casual and distant relationship. It means hanging out where they are, entering into their interests and passions, becoming involved in their problems and concerns. It means we don't just throw out a life ring; we take the risk of jumping in with struggling, drowning people. In the incarnation this is what Jesus does with us, and in following him we learn to do the same.

Sacrifice

Jesus calls us, along with his disciples, to follow his example (John 20:19–21):

> On the evening of that day, the first day of the week, the doors being locked where the disciples were for fear of the Jews, Jesus came and stood among them and said to them, "Peace be with you." When he had said this, he showed them his hands and his side. Then the disciples were glad when they saw the Lord. Jesus said to them again, "Peace be with you. As the Father has sent me, even so I am sending you."

The resurrected Jesus showed the disciples his hands and his side, revealing the wounds he received when he was crucified. Picture Jesus on the cross—bloody, bruised, and taking his last breath. Now listen to Jesus' words to you: "As the Father has sent me, even so I am sending you." He is calling us to be ready to die for the people we are reaching out to. Though most of us will not be required to give up our lives as Jesus' witnesses, there will be a kind of death involved. When we give of our time, money, and possessions, that is a sacrifice on our part. When we carry others' burdens, a sort of dying is involved. Have you ever noticed that when you talk to someone who is carrying a lot of burdens, at the end of the conversation they feel better and you feel drained? That's because you have begun to carry those burdens with that person. This is an example of the sacrifice Jesus is calling us to: living with the willingness to carry our neighbor's burdens because that is what Christ has done for us. We go with the posture of asking, "How can I give of myself for you?"

How can you engage in sacrificing for the people you are reaching out to?

Gospel Summary

We are citizens of heaven living on earth, pointing our friends, family, neighbors, and coworkers to the truth of a greater world made possible through Christ. We are appointed to go to those whom God has put into our lives, building relationships with them by sacrificially entering into their world. We have the power to do this in Christ, who left the comfort of his home with the Father and came to be with us. We can't keep from going to others because he came to us. We can't hold back from immersing ourselves in the world of those around us because he immersed himself in our world. We can't refrain from sacrificing and serving because Christ has become the suffering servant who gave his life for us.

Go, as Christ has come to you.

Discussion, Prayer, Application

1. At this point you might want to make an assessment of how many people God has put in your life with whom you can be building relationships. Some of you might find that you have a lot of friends who don't know Jesus, and some of you might find that you don't have many friends who don't know Jesus. I would suggest the following:

   If you find that you have a lot of friends who don't know Christ, start being intentional, together as a community, to build relationships with them (the next session will cover this in more detail).

   If you find that you don't have many friends who aren't Christians, find a neutral place where you can hang out, together as a community, and build some relationships with the people there. For example, you might

   - start gathering at a coffee house once a week to build relationships with people.
   - join a sports league.
   - start hanging out at a restaurant/bar. (Use wisdom here; you may find a lot of people who don't know Christ, but in going together as a community you will need to help each other remain distinct. Also, if someone in your group struggles with alcohol, this probably isn't a good idea.)
   - be creative and ask for God's direction to a place where he may want you to bring his presence.

Discuss and pray together about what your next step should be. Discuss possibilities and also potential problems.

2. Who are some people God has put in your life who don't know Christ? How can you be praying for them?

3. How is God calling you to enter into their world? Can you do this together as a community?

4. How is God calling you to sacrifice for the people he has put in your life?

5. How does the gospel empower you and set your motives right for reaching out to others?

Session 14

INVITE

BY DAVID HANCOCK

An Environment of Inviting

Our goal in this session is to equip your community to invite and welcome people who don't know Christ, just as Christ has done for you, into a community of hospitality, love, and joy. In community you can create an environment where your non-Christian friends can feel welcome so that they can experience a community that displays the gospel. In this way evangelism becomes a communal effort rather than an individual effort.

The communities immersed in the gospel on mission at our church have what we call an "open door dinner." They have dinner once a week at someone's house, and everyone is free to invite anyone they want. We eat together, pray before the meal, and simply enjoy each other's company. In this way our invited friends, family, neighbors, and coworkers can observe Christian community. This is the same kind of experience God desired for strangers within the ancient community of his people, as we learn in Leviticus 19:34: "You shall treat the stranger who sojourns with you as the native among you, and you shall love him as yourself, for you were strangers in the land of Egypt: I am the Lord your God."

At an "open door dinner" we might have conversations about God, but the main purpose of this time together is to create a welcoming atmosphere for all. While this may not seem particularly productive from an evangelistic point of view, it has actually been one of the most evangelically productive things we have done. This is really the beginning of evangelism as a community and is a vital step that is often missing. Here we are able to get to know the people we are reaching out to, learn how they might best be receptive to the gospel, and show them our love and care.

Many Christians have a desire to evangelize, but they don't know how to go about it. This kind of informal get-together allows for loving relationships to be built, and it creates an environment in which Christians can learn how to develop loving relationships with the intention of one day speaking the gospel to people who aren't Christians.

What does this environment of inviting look like?

- It is hospitable.
- It is loving.
- It is a joyful celebration.

Hospitable

Hospitality is an essential part of evangelism. Jeff Vanderstelt points out that the original Greek word for "hospitality" in the Bible is *philoxenia*, which means "love of strangers" (see Rom. 12:13; Heb. 13:1-2). He adds that "biblical hospitality is about making space for strangers," and he maintains that "home is our place of ministry." Our homes are not just our place where we escape to; they are the place where we welcome others in for the sake of the gospel. In his book *A Christian View of the Church* Francis Schaeffer says,

> Don't start a big program. Don't suddenly think you can add to your church budget and begin. Start personally and start in your home. I dare you. I dare you in the name of Jesus Christ. Do what I am going to suggest. Begin by opening your home for community . . . You don't need a big program. You don't have to convince your session or board. All you have to do

> is open your home and begin. And there is no place in God's world where there are no people who will come and share a home as long as it is a real home.

Our homes are our place of ministry, where we bring together both the Christian community and those we are building relationships with. When we start to see our homes as our place of ministry, we start to see that our houses, food, and things that we own are not actually ours to keep but what God has given us to share and even give away to others.

Loving

We invite people into our home not only to give and share what we have with them. We invite them also in order to love them. Our text makes clear that God wants us to have love not only for people in our community but also for those who are not believers. Today this means we welcome them in and love them as we love ourselves and others in the Christian community.

Earlier we said that a community that is "shaped by the gospel" is a community of genuine love and humility, a community that brings itself low in order to lift others up. We are called also to extend the same humble love to the people we are inviting in. When Jesus ate his last meal with the disciples before his death, he brought himself low and washed their feet (John 13:1-17). He told his disciples that his action was a picture of the humility, service, and sacrifice they should display to others.

Genuine love forgets itself. It is willing to serve without being served in return. It is willing to find the good qualities in others and let them know about it without calling attention to oneself. It is willing to sacrifice time and energy for others without asking for anything in return. And it does all this with joy.

Joyful Celebration

Christian community is a community of joyful celebration. Because we have been brought out of the slavery of sin and death and into freedom with God, we have the most to be joyful for, and the most to celebrate.

In *A Meal with Jesus,* Tim Chester says that Christians "should have a reputation for throwing the best parties." It's not because we have the money to throw the best parties. It's not because we have the cleanest house. It's not because we have the best resources for entertaining. It's because we have a joy that can only be found in Christ. We should know how best to celebrate because we have the most to celebrate. Inviting people in is about inviting people into the celebration we are having because we are now free. Celebrate as a community, and let the people you are reaching out to be invited to the party.

Gospel Intentionality

In *Total Church,* Tim Chester and Steve Timmis point out, "Most gospel ministry involves ordinary people doing ordinary things with gospel intentionality." We are hospitable because we too were strangers who have been welcomed in and have been given a room by Jesus himself (John 14:2). Jesus came from his home with the Father in order to welcome us in. He came into our world, shared our lives, and sat at table with sinners. He now calls us to that same "incarnational" ministry.

Discussion, Prayer, Application

1. What can you do together to create an environment where you can invite your friends, family, neighbors, and coworkers into the Christian community? Discuss the following together:
   - what this will look like (meals, prayer, etc.)
   - where it will be
   - when it will be

   Take some time to pray about this and for the people you will invite.

2. What will be your biggest challenge in inviting people into your homes and seeing your homes as a place of ministry?

3. Be willing to serve without being served in return. Be willing to make others look better than you. Find the good qualities in others and let them know about it without calling attention to yourself. Be willing to sacrifice your time and energy for others without asking for anything in return. Is this something you struggle with? In what ways has Jesus already done these things for you? How does that empower you to do these things for others?

4. Is your community joyful? Do you know how to celebrate? In what ways does the gospel call for celebration in your community?

Session 15

TELL

BY DANA ALLIN

Positive on Jesus, but Not the Church

"I would go to a church if it cared about the world the same way Jesus did." I heard those sad words from a young man who, like many others who shared his feelings, had left the church. The title of Dan Kimball's book *They Like Jesus, But Not the Church* captures the reality that many sociologists and others of us have observed from today's culture: People like what they see in Jesus, but they don't think the church is reflecting the nature and call of Jesus. And often they are right.

That does not mean we should try to remake Jesus into a figure our culture might find acceptable, or to manipulate his teachings in order to affirm cultural norms. At the same time, we need to understand that the culture already often has a positive view of Jesus but does not have a positive view of the church. That may be part of the reason we find fewer people coming to church on Sunday mornings looking for answers. From even these general observations, we can see it is increasingly important for Christians to be trained and ready to share their faith outside of the church context.

Let's look at the challenge of creating open Bible studies as subsets of our missional communities into which we can invite Christians and non-Christians to study together the authentic truth of Christ. As we do this, we will need to keep three principles in mind that Jesus himself used when he invited people to come and see who he was in the process of giving their lives to him. We can also use these principles in individual conversations with people as they consider following Jesus.

Principle 1: Disrupt Preconceived Notions

At a recent mission conference, I was captivated by the keynote message from Carl Medearis, who has done phenomenal evangelism work among Muslims in the Middle East. He relayed a story about a time when he was speaking to undergraduates at Harvard. His opening sentence was "I am going to assume that you are all for the things that Jesus is for." And the people began to heckle and boo him. His response was "Well, I am sorry. I thought you were all for women's equality, caring for the poor, and freeing people from oppressive governments." As they nodded their heads in agreement, he said, "Well, Jesus is for those things as well."

The unbelieving culture has many preconceptions about Christians and the church. If we can disrupt preconceived notions, people may begin to open their minds to seeing the real Jesus. Jesus himself did this. In the story of the woman at the well in John 4, the Samaritan woman asked Jesus a question about the true place of worship, an issue that caused tension between Jews and Samaritans. She assumed Jesus' Jewish stance on the issue, but his response surprised her. He explained that neither paradigm offered a correct understanding of the true nature of worship. True worship is not about where a person worships God; it's about where the person's heart is in relation to God.

Without compromising the truths of our faith, it's always helpful when we can find ways of expressing our faith that destroy the preconceptions of our culture. A friend of mine was seeking to live intentionally for Christ in the midst of a local cigar shop. Lots of people in the shop knew him personally, and several also knew he was a Christian. He was reading in a chair, and a few individuals nearby were talking about abortion. Part of the way through the conversation one of them looked at my friend and said, "Well, we know you are pro-life because you are a Christian." They were correct about his belief, but instead of simply agreeing, he wanted to disrupt their preconceived ideas. So he responded, "Yes, I am pro-life, but I believe the challenge of the church will be to be more fully pro-life than merely against abortion. We as the church need to be more willing to be proactive in financially supporting and caring for pregnant mothers. We need to be more willing to adopt children—especially those of other ethnicities and those with physical challenges."

Of course, for most Christians this would not be news, but the cigar-store friends had assumed that Christians were simply against abortion. This opened up a great conversation for my friend to engage in the teachings of Jesus to welcome children and care about those who can't care for themselves. He took the opportunity to disrupt their thinking even though they were correct about where he fundamentally landed on this issue.

When we have the privilege of witnessing to the truth about Jesus, it's important to find ways that allow the disruptive nature of Jesus' teachings to challenge the preconceived ideas of those who do not yet know the Lord.

Principle 2: Ask Questions

One of the things I am involved with is life/ministry/professional coaching. Coaching involves the art of asking great questions and engaging in reflective listening. Good coaches never tell people things that they can discover for themselves. This simple truth has been helpful not only in formal coaching relationships but also in a variety of other relationships. It is exhilarating to see ministry teams, small groups, staff, and also friends and family members discover information and strategies in response to a few probing and insightful questions.

Jesus was a master at asking probing questions to get people to think about their lives and discover the truth:

- “Who do people say that the Son of Man is?” (Matt. 16:13).
- “What do you think about the Christ? Whose son is he?” (Matt. 22:42).
- “Why do you call me good?” (Mark 10:18).

Probing questions can be particularly helpful within a mixed Bible study group of believers and prospective believers. For example, in exploring Luke 18:18-25 about the rich young ruler, rather than hammering in the “moral of the story,” a simple question like this can open up a more fruitful conversation: “How do our material possessions get in the way of what might matter most?” Christians and non-Christians can easily discuss this type of question because they both struggle with it, and it can open up great dialogue about what is really important in life. Or, in examining the John 8 passage about the woman caught in adultery, some thought-provoking questions might be

- What about the man she was caught with? Why wasn’t he brought in for judgment?
- How might the woman’s husband have felt about Jesus’ verdict?
- In what other situations was Jesus more inclined to rebuke and blame those who broke the law?

Questions like these can help people begin to explore Jesus for who he is. They can also help us reflect on the church and whether it has been in line with or out of step with the actual nature of Jesus.

Principle 3: Take One Step at a Time

People sometimes assume that effective evangelism means presenting the core of the good news as quickly as possible to get people to make a decision for Christ. While we certainly don’t want to postpone presenting the good news out of fear or embarrassment, we also don’t want to force it in a way that makes someone feel we are pushing it down their throat. There are a couple of motivations for wanting people to make decisions quickly. One is a good motivation of wanting to see that people are saved. Another that is not so good, however, is that of falsely assuming that discipleship doesn’t happen until conversion.

The reality is that as people walk down the road of exploring Christ, discipleship is happening even before they make a formal declaration to follow Jesus. By not pushing decisions too early, people will gain a more complete view of Jesus and have a richer relationship with him when they commit to follow him.

It's interesting to see that in the gospels Jesus doesn't ask for a commitment from the disciples until midway through his relationship with them. He wants to make sure they know who he is before they make a commitment to him. It's also interesting that people often ask Jesus what they must do to receive salvation in comparison to his telling people that they need to be saved. The best evangelistic outcome of an open Bible study would be that through the exploration of the life of Jesus, people would begin to ask on their own, "How might I be saved? How can I receive forgiveness too?"

Reflection Questions

1. When have you had good conversations about Jesus with people who don't profess faith in him? What are the dynamics and situations that lead to good conversations about Christ? What are the dynamics and situations that lead to awkward or tense conversations about Christ?

2. Where do you see the three principles of conversation at work in Jesus' ministry? Where do you see these principles being applied by others in the New Testament? When have you seen Christians live out these principles when connecting with people who aren't Christians?

3. The three principles are certainly not exhaustive of the way Jesus interacted with people who did not profess faith in him. What are some other principles at work in the life and ministry of Jesus as he engages people with the truth of the gospel?

4. Think of all the people who don't profess faith in Jesus that you might invite to an open Bible study. Which ones might be more receptive, and which ones might be less receptive?

5. How would you go about inviting people to a Bible study that was a mixture of Christians and non-Christians? What types of things might you say to make the invitation? How would you respond to and follow up with people who are not receptive to the invitation?

6. What understandings or guidelines would you suggest for Christians who participate in a Bible study that includes a mixture of Christians and non-Christians? What guidelines would you suggest for all participants? How would you communicate these things to the various participants?

Prayer

Along with sharing prayer requests, pray together for persons whom you might invite in the future to an open Bible study.

Application

During the coming week, prepare questions on the following passages that you might use in a group that includes a mixture of Christians and people who do not profess faith in Jesus.

- the prodigal son story (Luke 15:11-32)
- the parable of the two men who approach God at the temple (Luke 18:9-14)

Session 16

BUILD

BY DANA ALLIN

A Trend Toward Accountability

I began working in youth ministry in the late 1990s, a time when student accountability groups were the big new thing in youth ministry. This was a good shift, since many youth groups, like churches, had a wide range of spiritual maturity among the students. For those students who were more committed, accountability groups became an important way for them to remain faithful to Jesus in the midst of the pressures and influences they faced in high school.

These were made up of three to five people of the same gender. Group members committed to be as honest as possible with one another regarding their various struggles with temptation as well as their desires to have consistent quiet time. These were great groups, and I saw what appeared to be a lot of maturity in the lives of the students who participated.

After a while, however, a major shortcoming became evident: while producing positive changes in behavior, the accountability groups didn't root change more deeply in students' hearts. The problem was that the motivation for behavioral change was not from the heart but rather out of a desire to "be good." It was a subtle yet very profound difference.

Many of the students in these groups were high achievers in school. They took advanced placement courses, were involved in competitive athletics, and engaged in other extracurricular activities. They wanted to excel at their activities—and that included youth group. They also wanted to be better Christians than everyone else, and they wanted their Christian achievements to be noticed by others. While this wasn't always the case, a sort of "competitive Christianity" became an unwelcome result.

One might say, "Well, at least they had behavior that was in line with what Jesus desired even if the motivation was off a little bit." But the more dangerous possibility was that the accountability groups were actually working against the dynamics of the gospel in the lives of these students. Since the students were motivated to "be good" by appealing to the pride of achievement, the groups may have been creating patterns of dysfunction rather than growing in the grace of Christ.

Accountability in the Early Church

In his letters to churches, Paul often addresses two very distinct groups. On the one hand he addresses Gentiles, who tended to see the good news of God's grace as a license to continue in their ingrained patterns of sin. On the other hand, he addresses the Jews, who tended to view their religion as a checklist in righteous living. Neither approach was in line with the message of the gospel. The gospel says that as we come to know, in the depths of our hearts, the reality of God's forgiving grace and the reality of our adoption by the Father in Christ, our lives will begin to reflect that new reality.

In Romans 12:1-2 Paul says, "I appeal to you therefore, brothers, by the mercies of God, to present your bodies as a living sacrifice, holy and acceptable to God, which is your spiritual worship. Do not be conformed to this world, but be transformed by the renewal of your mind, that by testing you may discern what is the will of God, what is good and acceptable and perfect." Paul is addressing both Jews and Gentiles here. The Jews are in danger of conforming to rule-based approval by which they seek to do the right things for the wrong reason, and the Gentiles are tempted to misunderstand the gospel as a license to continue in sin. Both groups need to be continually renewed in their mind.

Paul offers the sole basis for this renewal in the very first sentence: "By the mercies of God." The "mercies of God" are what Paul has been writing about in the preceding chapters of Romans. Even though "all have sinned and fall short of the glory of God" (Rom. 3:23), God has adopted us in Christ Jesus on the basis of his works, not ours. As a result, we have a new Father, and we are to live out of the depth of that truth rather than by other false, temporal perceived realities.

Refocusing Accountability Today

Gospel accountability groups today differ from the 1990s accountability groups by focusing on this all-important foundation in "the mercies of God." A gospel accountability group, like the earlier groups, is made up of three to five people of the same gender. But instead of simply looking at what they are doing wrong, the group members seek to identify idols and false gods in their lives that influence not only incorrect behavior but also "good behavior" that might be sinfully motivated. Then the group can speak the truth of the gospel into those various situations.

For example, let's say that a person is having a difficult time forgiving someone who has wronged them. Instead of simply urging the person to forgive the other, a gospel accountability group will focus on the forgiveness that the person has experienced deep in their own heart "by the mercies of God." That will give the motivation and strength to work toward true forgiving. Forgiveness is not just a matter of obligation as "the right thing to do"; instead, it is rooted in the personal experience of forgiveness in Christ.

Similarly, if a person in the group struggles with greed and personal gain, then instead of simply condemning the greed and urging faithful giving, a gospel accountability group will work toward a personal understanding of the generosity of Christ. By personally internalizing Jesus' generosity, a way is opened for a new freedom of giving, motivated by the Holy Spirit, to pour out of the person's life.

Another person might struggle with an inappropriate motivation for volunteering in the church, tempted by a hidden desire for recognition. The gospel accountability group can work to help that person see that their infinite worth is already secured in Christ. That can free them to serve out of joy rather than out of a desire to gain fame or public approval.

Gospel accountability groups also help people with discernment. A person may be deciding on whether or not to continue in a dating relationship. The group's discussion can center on the motivations for the relationship and help the person discern whether motives that are not centered in the gospel might be at work.

A gospel accountability group is also vitally important to ensure that we continue to participate in God's mission in the world with the incarnational posture of Christ. We can easily be drawn into the temptation of being complacent, and we can make every logical excuse for not joining in God's mission in the world. Sometimes we can even engage in God's mission with a selfish motivation. A gospel accountability group helps to test our motives and to stir us toward greater action that is developed through understanding the gospel.

Warning: It could be tempting to write off the gospel accountability group as unnecessary. But in order for your community to really thrive, there must be the element of gospel accountability.

Reflection and Discussion

1. Sometimes the concept of an accountability group has a negative connotation. What are some of the negative connotations or abuses of accountability groups? How do you make sure your groups do not take on those characteristics?

2. Look back to session 9 on speaking the gospel. How do the principles associated with speaking the gospel help you understand the nature of how gospel accountability groups function?

3. Proverbs 27:17 uses an image that describes persons sharpening one another as "iron sharpens iron." How is that image helpful in understanding the way we interact with one another in gospel accountability groups?

4. Read 1 Thessalonians 2:1-12. Paul recounts the ministry that the team has had with the Thessalonians.
   a. What are the ways in which Paul and the ministry team nurtured the church with the gospel? Which examples stand out prominently to you?

   b. In verse 12 Paul mentions "encouraging, comforting and urging you to live lives worthy of God" (NIV). What are the differences between these actions? Why are all three actions needed in gospel accountability?

5. Paul says in Romans 12:1-2 that we are not to be conformed to the world but to be transformed by the renewing of our minds. In what ways are you tempted to be conformed to the world? After a person shares about their struggle in a particular area, invite the group to *encourage, comfort, and urge* that person with the truth of the gospel.

Prayer

Along with sharing individual prayer requests, pray that as your missional community takes shape, you will have the courage and willingness to engage in authentic gospel accountability.

Application

As you look forward to forming a gospel accountability group, write down some elements that you would like to see as part of a covenant among the members of the group. Also think of some foundational questions you would want to ask one another to facilitate gospel community.

PUTTING IT ALL TOGETHER

Session 17

COOPERATIVE LEADERSHIP IN MISSIONAL COMMUNITIES

BY DANA ALLIN

A Biblical Pattern—APEST

During this study, you most likely have had one person as the primary leader or facilitator of your group. Now, as the study draws to a close, it's important to think about the ongoing leadership of the group. While there may be one or two people who would seem to be likely candidates to take on the primary leadership, a missional community should ideally have a broader leadership base. This is not simply to spread the work around. It is rather to allow a biblical pattern of leadership development to emerge in your community.

The leadership pattern we advocate is found in Ephesians 4:11, and this is helpfully explained in Alan Hirsch's book *Permanent Revolution*. The five leadership offices—or roles, as we will refer to them here—are Apostle, Prophet, Evangelist, Shepherd, and Teacher (APEST). Typically these five roles have been minimized, dismissed, or distorted within the church. We minimize them by first thinking that only a few of these roles are active today. For example, in the

Reformed and Presbyterian traditions we tend to dismiss the roles of apostle and prophet as no longer applicable. The role of evangelist tends to be relegated to a few Billy Graham-types. On top of that, we tend to think that the roles that are still active are present only in our ordained clergy.

To grasp the nature of New Testament leadership, it's important to recognize that this letter of Paul is addressed not just to a few individuals or teachers but to the *whole* church at Ephesus and probably to the other churches nearby in Asia Minor. Notice, for example, how Paul talks about the unity of the whole body of Christ in Ephesians 4:4-6: "There is one body and one Spirit—just as you were called to the one hope that belongs to your call—one Lord, one faith, one baptism, one God and Father of all, who is over all and through all and in all." Paul also emphasizes in verse 7 that each member of the entire body of Christ is given a gift, and that the gifts are for the growth and maturity of the whole body. Clearly, Paul indicates that these roles are given to the whole body of Christ. Everyone is responsible for building up everyone else in love.

There will certainly be times when a trained and ordained person is responsible to fill a role or do a task, but this passage does not indicate that a few people equip everyone else for the work of the church. Christ's call is about the whole body building one another up in Christ.

We see these five leadership gifts as *roles* that provide the framework for shared leadership within the body of Christ. All the members of the body have at least one of the gifts described here, and all are called on to use them for the building up of the body.

Certainly each person will have a particular skill level and spiritual maturity that will indicate the breadth and the extent to which that role can be offered. For example, let's say God has given a new believer the gift of teaching. That person is probably not going to be a master teacher right away but will grow in that teaching role as skill, maturity, and understanding develop. Even Apollos, who was quickly recognized as a gifted teacher and speaker about Christ and the Scriptures, needed further direction and instruction (see Acts

18:24-26). Similarly, a person gifted in shepherding (encouragement, guidance, ongoing spiritual care) may need further training in putting the gift into practice.

Understanding leadership in the Christian community as a collective endeavor enables it to grow in a healthy environment in which everyone is gifted and responsible for using their gifts in roles that promote maturity, "to the measure of the stature of the fullness of Christ" (Eph. 4:13).

Let's look at each of these five roles to see how they work together to form and shape the missional community.

Apostle

Paul and the original disciples of Jesus were all called apostles. That led many interpreters to think that the role ceased in the church after these early leaders died. However, a close look at the New Testament shows that a number of others were also designated as apostles. Many in the church today are questioning the biblical basis for thinking that this role has ceased. Also, some traditions have made an opposite mistake, placing apostolic figures in a grandiose light above everyone else in the church. The word *apostle* simply means "sent one." The apostles are the ones who push the missional community or church into new territories for Christian witness. They can also be the people who start new things, the entrepreneurs of the church.

Prophet

Prophecy is often thought of as speaking about something in the future or in the past that has been revealed by God. But the role of the prophet in Scripture is primarily to speak God's Word to his people in their time and place, and especially to call them back from complacency and following the status quo to redirect them to the true heart and mission of God. Those with the role of prophet can sometimes be seen as annoying or critical within established churches or communities, but it is important to make sure these voices are heard within the community.

Evangelist

Evangelists are adept at sharing the truth of the gospel with unbelievers in a way that helps to lead to their transformation. Although this role is often seen as operating mainly "out in the world" and outside the community, evangelists serve within the community to keep people focused on their missional purpose, and evangelists help fellow Christians by reminding them of the gospel. They also serve by helping believers who struggle with doubts and by speaking the gospel afresh to members of the body who are overcome by sin.

Shepherd

Shepherds are often thought of as caregivers, but their role goes much further. The shepherd walks with people along the path of discipleship, especially in watching and observing what the Holy Spirit is doing in their lives. This helps in the discernment of next steps for a person's growth in discipleship. During times of difficulty in people's lives, the shepherd will also find ways to comfort and encourage them, using that opportunity to strengthen them and help them grow in faith and maturity as disciples of Jesus Christ.

Teacher

The teacher imparts biblical truth and protects individuals as well as the entire body from heresy and apostasy. The teacher might have the formal venue of the pulpit in a church, but many others carry out this role in small groups, classrooms, and in everyday conversations about faith in Christ. We all need to grow in understanding the gospel, and teachers of all kinds and in all sorts of settings facilitate that growth.

How It All Works Together

A missional community may or may not have a particular person designated as the overall leader of the group. But even if the group has a designated leader, it is important to ensure that all members are able to use and develop their gifts/roles to the extent of their ability/maturity in faith.

In a healthy missional community, with each person fulfilling his or her role, different people will take the lead in different situations. A person with the apostolic role will be thinking, praying, and working on how the community will prepare to multiply itself and expand into new areas for the gospel. But that same person doesn't have to be the Bible study leader. Several roles (probably teacher, prophet, evangelist, and possibly all five) may be needed for any Bible study session, especially if the study group includes Christians and non-Christians. An evangelist or teacher may also take up the primary leadership of a group meeting. A shepherd or prophet might lead the gospel accountability group. Each individual will lend his or her leadership to the growth and development of the missional community in order to develop a mature group that is balanced by all the leadership roles. An evangelist or an apostle might bring someone new into the community who is not yet a believer. But it may be through the work of a shepherd, teacher, or prophet that the person comes to faith and trust in Christ.

Ephesians 4:15-16 gives a beautiful picture of what the missional community will look like when everyone is fulfilling the role to which God has called them. Paul says, "Speaking the truth in love, we are to grow up in every way into him who is the head, into Christ, from whom the whole body, joined and held together by every joint with which it is equipped, when each part is working properly, makes the body grow so that it builds itself up in love."

May our communities be a reflection of the body of Christ as God intended!

Reflection and Discussion

1. Although the Apostle, Prophet, Evangelist, Shepherd, and Teacher (APEST) roles are to be used within the body of Christ, in what ways do you see parallel functions working in groups outside of the church, such as in businesses, civic organizations, or even informal interactions?

2. Think about each of the APEST roles. What are some examples from Scripture about people fulfilling each role? Think about and describe some ways in which people with different roles worked together for God's purposes.

3. Which of the APEST roles do you feel you have, and why? (You may wish to take an APEST typology inventory at www.apest.org. You can do this as a self-assessment, or you can sign up for a 360-degree evaluation in which others can give input as well.)

4. If all believers have one of these roles (whether it is fully developed or in its infancy stage), how can being in a missional community help individuals use their gifts more freely than they could in a traditional, established church?

5. Take some time in your group to preliminarily identify the roles/gifts that each member might have. How have you seen these individuals live out these roles in small or large ways?

6. Which roles tend to be more prominent in your group, and which are less prominent? How can you make sure that as your group develops, all roles are active and the group is balanced?

7. During this study you have seen some of the different elements that develop within a missional community, such as Bible study with believers and non-believers, gospel accountability groups, and open door events as entry points into the community. Think about and discuss which people in your group might take or share the lead in each of these activities or events.

8. How can you gain greater clarity on what your particular role is? What things can you do to develop the ability to use your role?

Prayer

Along with sharing your prayer requests, ask God to continue to reveal each others' roles within your community.

Application

During the coming week, see how you might use your particular APEST typology and look for how the APEST roles are at work in others' lives.

Session 18

ORGANIC LEADERSHIP DEVELOPMENT

BY DANA ALLIN

Learning to Use Our Gifts

When I was in high school, a nearby Toyota dealer gave away a new car every year to a graduating senior from one of the three local high schools. Amazingly, I won a brand-new green Toyota Tercel, replacing my grandmother's Oldsmobile Cutlass Supreme (also known as "The Boat"). There was only one problem: when I got into the new car to drive it off the lot, I realized it had a stick shift (manual transmission). I had to have my mom drive the car off the lot for me—which, as you can imagine, was a little embarrassing for a high school senior. I was given a great gift, but I had to learn how to use it!

Winning that car reminds me of how God gives us spiritual gifts and roles to play in the missional community. We can be given these gifts, but we must learn how to use them within the body of Christ. In the previous session, we looked at the nature of leadership in the missional community and saw that leadership roles are given to all believers for use in various situations according to their APEST typology (Ephesians 4:11). Though God may have gifted and called a person to a particular role, he or she must fill that calling effectively—and that requires training and mentoring.

It is important, therefore, not only to identify gifts in the community but also to train people in the effective use of their gifts. Often this means that gifted leaders take the time and effort to develop and train others. The diagram below describes the process of gift development.

GIFTING	→	MINISTRY	→	LEADERSHIP
God has given the person a gift, but the person is not using the gift.		The person is using his or her gifts in ministry.		The person is training others to use their gifts.

While there are many wonderful books and other more extensive resources on leadership development, this session will look at several core principles to include as your community thinks about developing and multiplying leaders.

Develop the Whole Person—Heart, Head, and Hands

If I need emergency surgery, my main concern is to get the most skilled surgeon I can find, regardless of his or her personality or bedside manner. In the development of leaders in the Christian community, however, character needs to be built alongside skills and abilities. For example, a skilled but brash corporate leader who knows how to get things done may be destructive within the context of Christian community.

Leadership development in Christian communities involves "heart, head, and hands" (also referred to as "be, know, and do"). "Heart" development involves the spiritual maturity of the individual. Who is this person at their core? This is evidenced by the extent of the Christlike character and the fruit of the Spirit in the person's life.

But a good heart is not enough for effective leadership. The leader also needs knowledge and understanding. "Head" development points to the leader's knowledge base, not only in terms of biblical or theological knowledge but also in terms of the principles and practice of ministry.

Of course, the effective leader also needs skills and abilities, or "hands." Someone, for example, might have great theological or biblical understanding but may not be able to teach in a comprehensible way to others. Hebrews 5:11-14 addresses the development of the head and the hands. In this passage the author exhorts people who have become dull in understanding. They are still in need of milk when they should be able to digest solid food; by this time in their Christian journey, they should have become teachers rather than remaining mere listeners. The writer is therefore addressing their need for more head knowledge as well as the fact that they should be "doing" the teaching of others.

Give Nickel Jobs First

When I first became a church pastor, I was 25 years old, and the average age of the church members was 75. Wanting to draw more young families into the congregation, we invited a couple of younger members to be on the session (congregational council), and one of them was selected and ordained to office. It turned out to be a mistake. We didn't heed the warning of 1 Timothy 5:22, which cautions against ordaining someone to a leadership role too quickly.

Later someone described our mistake this way: "You gave someone a dollar job before he had done nickel jobs." Jesus' parable of the talents in Matthew 25:14-30 powerfully illustrates this principle. Each of the servants is entrusted with an amount according to their ability. The problem with giving people responsibility too quickly is that it can frustrate the developing leader as well as those whom they try to lead and serve.

In the case of that congregation, I think that the person we ordained too quickly eventually could have developed into a great elder. However, by giving him that responsibility too quickly, both he and others became frustrated, and eventually he dropped out of leadership and then out of the church altogether. Ever since that experience, I have used a "nickel, dime, quarter, dollar" concept with staff, leaders, and nominating committees in order to make sure we move people forward in ministry responsibility in line with their development of gifts.

In the process of developing leaders, it is important to think about where they currently are in their development and how we can encourage them to grow without breaking them. This is especially important in missional communities. Since you will want to embrace the goal of multiplying leaders and groups fairly quickly, it may be a temptation to give too much responsibility too soon.

Action and Reflection

After Jesus sent out seventy-two followers to announce, "The kingdom of God has come near," he later gathered them so that they could process their experiences together (see Luke 10:1-24). It is important to give people the opportunity to reflect on their ministry experiences. If someone is taking their first steps in using their APEST typology, they will often make mistakes. Sometimes their mistakes will be significant. It is important, therefore, to reflect with the person on what went well and what might need improvement in the future. The reflection phase is a great opportunity to address again the development of the whole person and to discern where they might need to grow in knowledge, skills, or character.

Training Is a Process

There is a saying that I think originated in the training of doctors: "Watch one, do one, teach one." When doctors are learning a skill, they need to first watch someone who has experience using that skill. They are then to practice the skill themselves. Finally, when they have learned the skill well, they can teach someone else to do it. In recent years while applying this principle to ministry, leaders and teachers have amplified the process into five steps.

"I do, you watch, we talk"—In this phase, the person being trained is free to observe and have a time of reflection.

"I do, you help, we talk"—In this phase, the person being trained participates in the task but doesn't have the primary responsibility for doing the task. Once the task is finished, the trainer and trainee reflect on it together.

"You do, I help, we talk"—In this phase, the person being trained takes the primary leadership in the task, but the trainer helps the person prepare for and execute the task. Once the task is complete, they take time to reflect together.

"You do, I watch, we talk"—In this phase, the person being trained does the whole activity from start to finish while the trainer observes the trainee in action. When the task is complete, they reflect on it together.

"You teach someone else, and we talk"—At this phase, the person who has been trained in a particular task has the responsibility to train someone else in the same task. The original trainer is now training the learner in how to train others. This aspect in leadership development is often overlooked but is vitally important if one is going to do more than train a few leaders and really be able to facilitate leadership multiplication.

Reflection and Discussion

1. Who have been the most influential people in your own growth in ministry?

2. The first principle of leadership development is to develop the whole person: heart (being or character), head (knowledge), hands (skills and abilities). In what ways might you need to grow in each of these areas?

3. What happens if a potential leader grows in one or two areas but not in all three? What examples have you seen of uneven growth like that? How can you help emerging leaders develop in all three areas? What examples in Scripture portray leaders who were unbalanced? What were some problems that resulted?

4. Read the parable of the talents in Matthew 25:14-30. What do we learn about the way in which God delegates ministry to his people? How can you apply these principles in your missional community?

5. Applying the Action and Reflection principle is important, but we must ensure that we give feedback in a constructive way rather than in a demoralizing way. We have talked about being gospel saturated in our lives. How do we bring gospel dynamics into our reflection with leaders in training?

6. Look at the final leadership development principle presented in this session (recommending a process of watching, doing, and reflecting). Why are all of the steps important? Why might some trainers hesitate to follow through with all of the steps?

7. Whom are you training? Whom should you be training? Who is training you? Whom might you approach to ask if they would train you further?

Prayer

In Matthew 9:35-38 Jesus teaches us to ask God to send workers into his harvest field. Spend some time praying that God will continue to develop you and others to help in his harvesting work.

Application

During the coming week, think more deeply about question 7. Make a list of a couple of people whom you could help to develop formally or informally. Also make a list of a couple of people who could help you grow in developing your heart, head, and hands for leadership.

Session 19

CONTEXT

BY JIM SINGLETON

Understanding Unique Contexts

In 1987 I was in northern Kenya working on a community development project. My goal was to train a group that could make visits throughout the village explaining the meaning of the gospel. My host missionary suggested that first we visit with the elders of the village, who should be informed of the project. I agreed that such a visit would be fine. As I sat down with the elders and a translator, the first thing the elders wanted to know about was my family. I wondered what this had to do with the project I had in mind.

The elders proceeded to tell me about their families and even how many cattle and goats they owned. Then they wanted to know how many cattle my father owned. Now I was really puzzled, since my father did not have any cattle. We were now on a topic far different from the project I wanted to discuss, lost in what seemed like irrelevant details about my family. Only later did I learn that in the tribal culture there individuals were seen mainly as pieces in a family and tribal system. I had to learn that I was in a different cultural context.

Similarly, as Christian communities, we need to be aware of our context. Congregations that were shaped by the Builder generation (born before 1946) amid "Christendom" ideas that were prevalent in the 1950s often have a difficult time understanding subsequent generations (Baby Boomers, Gen X, Millennials). Each generation has characteristics that make them like a different tribe of people. When we add variations of ethnicity and region, we find we are in even more complex contexts for communicating the gospel afresh. I have been a pastor in several regions of the United States, and each place hears the gospel differently. Without first understanding these unique contexts, we risk miscommunication and misunderstanding.

Adapting to Different Contexts

It's fascinating to see how the apostle Paul adapted to the local context in his visit to Athens (Acts 17:16-34). When he was invited to speak in the Areopagus, his strategy for sharing the gospel there was different than in other places. Paul had noticed that among the Athenians' many objects of worship (idols) there was even an altar dedicated "to an unknown God." It was probably a strategy of the Athenians to worship any gods whose names they did not know. In that Paul saw an opportunity to explain the good news of Jesus to a culture that had no background for relating to the Messiah of the Jews. The Athenians were interested in all kinds of new ideas, so Paul also used some well-known Greek poetry to begin to explain God's purposes in creating us and coming to save us. Because of the way Paul addressed them in terms of their own cultural and religious context, the people of Athens were intrigued by the news he shared about Jesus Christ.

The Challenge of Today's New Contexts

The Christian gospel has taken root more widely than any other world religion. It is present on every continent. It is growing rapidly in Africa and South America and thriving in places like South Korea and China. The missions movement has brought the gospel into nearly every culture on this planet. Now in North America we face the challenges of helping new generations and new subcultures hear the gospel afresh in their own words and ideas. For several decades we have watched a slow exodus from congregations as young adults have not been able to hear the gospel in a way that connects to their lives. Understanding context is the first step in helping congregations to engage the cultures around them. Too often we want "them" to just become like "us." But in the incarnation of Christ we see the pattern of Jesus becoming like us to bridge the gap between God and sinful humanity.

May our gospel communities use this whole study to begin the process of becoming who the Lord is sending us to be.

Reflection and Discussion

1. What part of the story in Acts 17 is new to you?

2. Assuming that Jesus wants us to engage with our context, what would be the most natural subculture for your gospel community to try to reach?

3. In what ways might your congregation or community seem incomprehensible to that subculture?

4. What adaptions could you make that would help to clarify the gospel to that subculture while not diminishing the essence of the gospel?

Prayer

After sharing a range of prayer requests, join in prayer and ask the Spirit for guidance in reaching a culture that needs to hear the good news in a way that connects with them today.

Application

Work together as a community to imagine how you can become more cross-cultural and then adapt to bring the good news of Jesus into another context.

Session 20

DEVELOPING A PLAN FOR YOUR MISSIONAL COMMUNITY

BY DANA ALLIN

Congratulations! You have completed the initial formation stage of your missional community. It has been our experience that when people find out that the missional community formation process takes about six months, they will push back and want a process that will be shorter, such as eight to ten weeks. That is certainly understandable; most programs and small group studies are designed to be that length. The formation of a missional community, however, is much more than a program or a Bible study. It involves more than acquiring new information ***with*** a group people; it is truly a reformation ***of*** a group of people.

What you have gone through is in some ways like basic training in the military. During basic training a person gains a new identity, new skills, new strengths, and a new family—all focused on a new purpose. And after basic training you continue to grow as you apply what you have learned and experienced.

Now that you have had your basic training, you understand your new identity in the gospel of Jesus Christ. You have new skills that you have begun to develop and practice through various exercises. The Spirit has reminded you of your new strength through the gospel and helps you apply that to your daily life. You have a new family that includes other brothers and sisters in Christ. You have a new mission to partner with God in his redemptive purposes in the world.

In this closing session you will discern the particular mission field(s) to which God is calling your community, and you will determine the best strategies and rhythms to use personally and communally for reaching those communities. Sometimes people will want to articulate a specific mission focus and would rather simply be open to where the Spirit might lead in a particular circumstance. It is certainly important to be aware of such opportunities and to be open to the Spirit's leading. However, if we follow the incarnational model, we see that Jesus spent the vast majority of his ministry in one area and that this produces the longest lasting and greatest fruit for the gospel.

Below are primary questions you and your group will need to answer, followed by some additional questions to stimulate the group's thinking. Answering these questions will help you articulate your mission. You might want to copy and complete a Missional Community Formation worksheet (see the pages following this session) for each of the potential groups with which you are thinking about interacting. See also our website, *flourishmovement.org,* for examples of missions and strategies for groups.

1. What is the community we are called to serve?

Remember that living missionally isn't so much about adding new things to your life, but about doing with gospel intentionality what you are already doing. Once you think about it, you will find that your group has at least three to five natural circles of influence where at least some of your members are involved. For example, you may have a group of people who have children in the same school or in the same extracurricular activity. Or some people in the group may live in the same neighborhood or may be part of the same civic club, book club, or other association. In addition, some might work or have worked in the same company or field; some might exercise at the same location or be part of a sports team; some might frequent a local pub or restaurant that has its own subculture. If you can't think of such places for interaction with others in the local community, you might be too insular and God may be calling you to take some intentional steps out into the surrounding community. The key question is, What are those communities with whom at least a few of you can naturally engage frequently and for an extended period of time?

2. What are some places in the local community where the gospel is naturally attractive or offensive?

If you study your community, you will find places where there is a natural resonance with the gospel message, and you will find places where the gospel brings resistance in connection with people's behavior and their approach to life.

For example, some people will really have a heart and desire to make the world a better place, but they may think that Christians don't care about these types of things. I have some family members who thought Christians don't care about the suffering in the world around us. They were shocked to hear about the way my church was not only feeding and clothing people but also treating people with dignity by helping them break out of the perpetual cycle of poverty. Ministries like this help people to change their perceptions and recognize that the gospel is in line with some of their desires.

But you will also find ways in which the gospel is naturally offensive to people's perspectives. You might also see some ways in which people are trying to fill the "God-shaped" hole that we all have in our lives. In some areas, work and achievement are the idols that make people feel important. In other cases, recreation is the idol with which people live to have fun and try to fulfill their natural yearnings for God. For others it is their family; for example, if their kids are successful, then they are fulfilled.

3. What are the natural rhythms and practices that you, individually and as a group, can use to engage and have proximity with this particular community?

By committing to particular rhythms and practices that give you proximity to the community to which God has called you, you will be creating an environment in which the Sprit can work in people's hearts and lives. Michael Frost in his book *Exiles* talks about individual and corporate missional rhythms to which you can commit. These are centered on the acronym BELLS:

- The *B* stands for *Bless:* In what way can you bless three people this week?
- The *E* is for *Eat:* Can you tithe your meals and spend three of them intentionally with the community around you?
- The first *L* stands for *Listen:* Can you listen one hour a week to what the Lord might be saying in your life?
- The second *L* is for *Learn:* Can you continually learn by being immersed in the Gospels at all times, along with other books of Scripture, to get the whole counsel of God?
- The *S* stands for *Sent:* Where have I partnered with and where have I resisted God's purposes in the world?

It is ideal to do these things individually and communally. A person therefore might commit to eating lunch or having coffee once a week with someone outside of their home and also invite people into their home. One member of a group was willing to have 20+ people over to their house every week, and that gave an opportunity for several of their members to interact with others in a social setting. Other people may simply commit to having another family or person over for dinner a couple of times a month. Some people work out together, or go to the beach together, or go out for coffee or a meal in connection with the flow of their group. See session 14 for more information.

4. How will people who are curious have an environment to explore?

Your community may not start off with a study geared for Christians and non-Christians. However, when God brings those opportunities, how will the group be prepared to interact? You might think of a few books that could spark good discussion. People have used in a more academic setting Tim Keller's *The Reason for God*; others have used Jen Hatmaker's book *7: An Experimental Mutiny Against Excess,* which doesn't address faith directly at first but presents consumerism as an entry point to talk about the gospel.

When you do a study, will you do it as a small group, one on one, or in some other format? It will be important to think about this in advance so that when opportunities arise, you will be prepared to engage more deeply. See session 15 for more information.

5. How will you grow with other believers?

In session 16 we talked about creating an environment in which groups of believers can continually immerse themselves in the gospel and speak the gospel to one another. It will be important for the group to identify the ways in which each of them will participate in these gospel accountability groups.

6. What are the various roles within Ephesians 4:11-12 that people in your group can play?

It will be important for everyone to have an understanding of what they bring to the shaping of the community. Ideally each person will have taken the APEST inventory (www.apest.org) to find out how God has begun to work through them. Certainly the use of those roles will depend on spiritual maturity and skills to assist in each person's calling, but it will be important to gain an idea about the most natural functions for the people in your group. See session 17 for more information.

MISSIONAL COMMUNITY FORMATION

INDIVIDUAL REFLECTION

As you begin to think about the mission and ministry of your missional community, it will be helpful to do some personal reflection that you can bring to a group discussion. Prayerfully think through these questions on your own, or with your spouse, to prepare for a group discussion.

1. What are the possible communities with which I/we could engage?

2. For each of these communities, in what areas will people naturally be attracted to the gospel, and where will the gospel be offensive?

3. What missional rhythms will you commit to personally or as a family? (See session 14.)

4. In what ways or with what material could you aim to help people who are seeking to process issues of faith? (See session 15.)

5. As you think about engaging in a gospel accountability group, who would likely be in that group with you? What commitments and covenants would you want to make with each other? (See session 16.)

6. Identify your primary and, if possible, your secondary APEST role that you can use within your missional community. In what ways do you need to grow in your ability to use these roles? (See session 17.)

MISSIONAL COMMUNITY FORMATION

GROUP REFLECTION

Each member or family within the missional community should have completed the preceding individual reflection. Prayerfully use this worksheet to compile your thoughts as a group and to crystallize the particular mission of your group.

1. What are the communities your group is called to reach? In what ways do these communities overlap with one another? In what ways are they separate?

2. For each of these communities, in what areas will people naturally be attracted to the gospel, and where will the gospel be offensive? How will this inform your mission strategy?

3. What missional rhythms will you commit to as individuals and as a group? (See session 14.)

4. As people begin to have an interest in matters of faith, how will your group engage more deeply with them? (See session 15.)

5. Who will make up the smaller groups that aim to grow deeper in faith and in gospel accountability together? (See session 16.)

6. Identify each member of the group's primary and secondary APEST roles. How can each person use his or her roles within the group? (See session 17.)